Cardboard Condo

Cardboard Condo

◆

How the Homeless Survive the Streets

Robert C. Greene

iUniverse, Inc.
New York Lincoln Shanghai

Cardboard Condo
How the Homeless Survive the Streets

Copyright © 2005 by Robert C. Greene

All rights reserved. No part of this book may be used or reproduced by any means, graphic, electronic, or mechanical, including photocopying, recording, taping or by any information storage retrieval system without the written permission of the publisher except in the case of brief quotations embodied in critical articles and reviews.

iUniverse books may be ordered through booksellers or by contacting:

iUniverse
2021 Pine Lake Road, Suite 100
Lincoln, NE 68512
www.iuniverse.com
1-800-Authors (1-800-288-4677)

ISBN: 0-595-33710-4

Printed in the United States of America

Contents

Introduction	ix
Advocate	1
BARBARA L.	1
The Homeless	5
LEE B.	5
ALEX L.	7
ROBERT B.	10
DONNA M.	12
DON O.	14
TOM H.	16
MICHELLE C.	18
CLIFF J.	20
BURN B.	22
JOHN M.	24
MELINDA W.	26
C.L.	28
KEN K.	30
JOHN D.	36
JANEEN.	38
MICHAEL D.	40
JACK P.	44
DON H.	47
HELENA T.	50
ROBERT Y.	52
ARCHI.	56

MICHAEL W.D. 59
STEPHANIE V. 64
BRUCE M. 66
TOM P. 70
SCOTT C. 73
MARIA H. 75
FREDERICK 77
DAVID R. 80
GARY P. 82
VALERIE 85
PAUL S. 89
KAZ M. 93
JAMES X. 96
LENNEA. 99
TONY. 101
GENO B. 104
JOE 109
RACHAEL R. 113
LARRY K. 118
CINDY 121
DON W. 124

Survivors 128
FRANCIS D. 128
WILLIE M. 130
NICK 131
WILLIAM B. 133
JANE D. 135
JOHN P. 137
DAVE W. 140
ROBERT H. 143

The Community 146

The Police 149

Summary..153
About the Author 155

Introduction

In an effort to enable the reader to experience homeless persons as real people, each a separate and unique individual, I interviewed many on the streets and in the shelters of Santa Monica, California, known for its homeless. Most, I found, sleep in doorways, parks, in cardboard make-do homes, a few in shelters; others, some, have managed to re-enter society.

Why do I care? Because I came dangerously close to being homeless myself.

When I was in my twenties I developed schizophrenia. I turned to drugs to shut out the voices. I did not want to live at home with my family, but I could not hold a job long enough to support myself. The homeless became my environment. I identified with them, especially those who as I were schizophrenic themselves. I often brought them off the street, overcrowding my tiny apartment, giving them a place to sleep.

But the voices wouldn't silence. One night in desperation I took a kitchen knife and sliced my throat. Blood spurted like a fountain. Miraculously it clotted and I took it as a sign that I was not meant to die. I called 911. They took me to the UCLA Neuro-Psychiatric Center.

Thanks to a wonderful psychiatrist, modern medicine, and above all supportive parents, I survived and am living a normal life.

◆ ◆ ◆

The poor man's wisdom is despised, and his words are not heard.
Ecclesiastes 9:16–200 BC

Advocate

BARBARA L.

The following is an interview I had with Barbara L. at her home in Pacific Palisades. She is a volunteer advocate for the homeless.

Q: Do you work everyday for the homeless?

B: I work once a week now, every Monday.

Q: How and why did you become involved with helping the homeless?

B: Um, well, at that time I had an Indian Guru who told everybody to do service to people. So I was looking around and I found this alcoholics place—the Clare Foundation. I volunteered at Clare and I really liked it. I met somebody at Clare who was doing something in the park for homeless people, and she needed volunteers. So I said, "Oh, I want to do that, I want to do that."

This park thing was at Palisades Park where they were feeding homeless people. The person that I knew started the whole thing. She saw an old lady once sitting on a bench on Wilshire Blvd. Waiting for the bus. She wasn't really waiting for the bus. She was a homeless person. My friend just got a bowl of soup and brought it to her, and the bag lady loved it so much.

My friend then saw these homeless people in the park. So every day she would make a pot of soup. She would go to the park and get a table and pour it into paper cups, and they'd line up and get the soup. Then she began to get volunteers that would help her. By the time she found me she was doing more food besides the soup. So she asked me if I would like to take over on Mondays and get to know the procedure. So I got some volunteers and we started looking around for food, and found restaurants that would help us. We got some pizza from Italian restaurants, and we would get left over spaghetti, and bakeries would give us rolls and sweet stuff. We just began to get food, and the homeless people began to come, and we had good food, so more and more homeless people would show up. Sometimes we'd run out.

As it began to grow, my friend got other people. We had people for Monday, people for Wednesday with a big hot meal. Meanwhile the number of homeless people grew and grew and grew. It grew so much that the City (laughs) told us to get out of the park because it interfered with the tourists and everything. The City said, "Come to the City Hall, and we'll give you the City Hall and you can have all the homeless people here." So we said ok, and began serving people at City Hall.

I want to back up a minute and just talk about three homeless people who are outstanding in my mind. When we were at the park, we began to have a hard time because we were getting a lot of drugs, and drug addicts and violence. We'd get gangs, young guys who would form gangs, and they were mean you know. They would steal and rob. It was scary. The Police never came to help us. I'd come up with a big carload of food. We had to carry the food from the car to the picnic table.

Well, these gang guys would run and help carry the food, but the food would disappear by the time it got to the tables. Plates full of cookies would be gone. I had a whole tray of pasta that was gone. Things would just be missing. And these guys were so rough that the homeless would be frightened by them. They wouldn't tell on them. They knew who was stealing but they were afraid. They were scary guys. And then we had a stabbing. Someone stabbed to death. And, oh God, here I am working with these people and I could be killed doing this! What am I doing? I had no protection.

About that time, the City of Santa Monica got worried. So they got volunteer and shelter people together and said they were going to teach us how to protect ourselves. They had a professional person come in. They had an all day workshop and they taught us how to protect ourselves. That didn't make me feel any better. I was still scared. I would be shaking by the time I got to the park with a car full of food. I'm asking myself why am I doing this? I should never, ever do this again.

Well, I met this big black guy named Terry, a big, strong guy. And Terry became our protector. He began to protect us from all these criminals and drunkards and stuff. That made me feel a lot better. If there was an altercation, the others would get on Terry's side. So we got several guys that would protect us. There were cold winds coming from the Ocean, and it would be freezing out there, and my hands would be like ice. I thought, "I'll never be able to serve this food." Terry, this big old guy, took off his gloves and said, "I want you to use my gloves." And I thought, Oh, God, how can I put on Terry's gloves? He probably hasn't had a bath in five years, never washed his hands. So I made some excuse, "Oh, they're too big for me" (laughs).

Then, one time one guy got angry at one of the volunteers and threw a plate of beans in her face. It splattered all over. It splattered on me. Terry said, "I'm gonna help you." He took out his wallet, and inside his wallet was a little white handkerchief, all folded up, and he said, "I want you to have this to wipe your hands on."—so sweet to me. So, I took it and wiped my hands off on it. He was so unselfish and so sweet. And we liked him so much that we got to where we were willing to pay him to help us, but he never took any money. He didn't want any. He didn't want to be committed. He didn't want a job. He wanted to be totally free.

Well, then we moved to City Hall. At that time we began to have like 350 homeless people. We had to get more food. We had 16 volunteers. More and more residences began to help us, and they brought a lot of food. We tried to help some of the homeless that we felt were really sincere. We tried to put them up for the night so they could at least take a shower. So they could have some sleep. We did that with a lot of them.

And we met Sylvester, who was a little guy (laughs fondly) who was 70 years old—a little black man. Sylvester had a lot of kin, and he had given all his money to his son who had a drug problem. He got thrown out of his apartment because he couldn't pay the rent, and had no place to stay. So he spent every night, all night long, on the buses. He would go back and forth from Santa Monica to Downtown LA on buses because he was scared to death to spend the night on the street. So, we put Sylvester up in a Hostel. Finally we found him an apartment in Santa Monica in a Senior building. We paid the first month's rent. Sylvester had a small pension. So we got him started, and he was able to stay in the apartment. He wanted to volunteer to help us, so we began to pay him fifteen dollars a week. I think we finally upped it to twenty dollars and then to fifty a week. To really help us out, people began donating money to us. Sylvester was a wonderful, wonderful help. He just devoted his life to helping the homeless people and helping us out. Sylvester was very religious, and he went to a Christian Church. He went there all the time. Very religious.

Meanwhile, what finally happened to Sylvester—in the Church was a man who directed TV commercials. Sylvester was so unusual, such a wonderful character, unusual looking, that the man asked him to come try out for a TV commercial. Which is what Sylvester did, and he got a Ford commercial. He was on these Ford commercials all the time. And then, from that, he did so many other commercials. Like Pepsi for instance. He had so many commercials going, he began to make money, and stopped taking money from us. But he always volunteered. He kept coming seven days a week to work with us. Eventually, not too long ago, he died of a heart attack. He was in his late 80s.

Q. What can people do to help the homeless?

B. Well, for one thing they can give to the shelters, like The Ocean Park Community Center that's open in the morning for anybody. We used to have cards we would hand out that would tell the homeless where to go to get food. I think there will always be homeless people—people that don't have anyone to support them. They don't want to go home. There's no place to go. It's really sad you know. I know some homeless people who are such wonderful people. I really like them. A lot of them want to be where they're at. They have freedom. They don't have to talk to anybody. They don't have to answer to somebody. There are others who want to get off the streets SO BAD. This shelter where I work really helps people to get off the street with jobs and programs. Out of a hundred people who live there we always have twenty to twenty-five percent of the people working jobs.

When I was working at the Oceanside Community Center there was a guy named Tony who was Asian/Indian. He was very religious. He was raised as a Hindu. But he got into the wrong gang, so his relatives wouldn't accept him anymore. They broke into various places, stole TVs. He was really a nice person, he cooked and he helped, but he couldn't get away from that gang. He was a sweetheart, but he just couldn't break away. I was going on a trip to India and he asked could I just bring him back one thing from Shiva. So, in India I found this little silver Shiva medal with a chain, real cheap. Oh, he loved it!

Well, the next time I saw him he didn't have the medal. It had been taken from him. He couldn't get away from that gang. Then he just disappeared, and I don't know what happened to him. You got guys like that, always getting in with the wrong people. Most of the homeless I like very, very much. They're my friends. I've had some friends for fifteen years that are still on the street. There are others that try and try to get out, but they can't. Some, that's where they want to be. It's strange, you know…

The Homeless

LEE B.

Lee is a fifty-seven year-old black man with a bristling grey and black beard. I met him at his shanty which is pictured on the cover. He had constructed his shanty out of spare wood, cardboard, blankets and painters' tarps. Inside there was a queen-size mattress covered with blankets. Everything was clean.

Q. How long have you been homeless, Lee?

L. About three years.

Q. What happened?

L. Well, I started looking for work but couldn't find no job. I had a bad relationship with my wife. I ended up going to jail. I had gotten an assault case out of it.

Q. Was it on your wife?

L. No, it was on this other guy who was with her. This was in February of 2000.

Q. This is a nice place you got here.

L. Before this place I was downtown, and the police were really messing with me. So I had to get out and move, you know. But I didn't have a place to stay. I was one of the first original people up here under this Freeway underpass. I just put all this together.

Q. Are you on welfare, or any other program?

L. No, I don't get either one. I was on SSI but they suspended me because I got a warrant in Portland, Oregon. After they suspended me I couldn't get GR (General Relief), I couldn't get food stamps. So, I became a fugitive. They found out I was a fugitive up here because I didn't finish my probation. I did all the other things but I just couldn't handle the probation. This was in '99. I had an apartment and everything. I was on SSI and I had everything going on. In the year 2000 they cut me off cause they found out I was a fugitive. I can't get no job because every time it happens they find out I'm a fugitive. The only money I get is by panhandling. I look forward to going back up to Oregon and getting back my SSI. Nobody would give me money for a ticket back up there, so here I am.

Q. Are there any places around here where you can go to eat?

L. I usually go to the hospital where I can get a full meal. Lunch trucks that come through here sometimes are pretty good. They help me out. People come around here every Monday, Wednesday and Friday. (He points to three bagels in a plastic bag tied to the fence.)

Q. So what's a typical day for you?

L. Well, a typical day I would get up whenever I get up, walk up on the streets, up on Pico and drink. Cause there's nothin' else to do. I know the guys up there so we just hang out and drink.

Q. Did you ever get in any fights here?

L. Yeah, I had about three of them. The first time this guy was trying to move in here. He had all sorts of people and they would come in here when I wasn't home and be shooting dope and stuff. He kind of fired on me so I kinda fired back on him. I was really angry cause this guy took all my cosmetics and stuff. I tried to hide it up under my mattress. They'd just come in and ransack everything. You can't have nothin' out here. There was another guy I was having trouble with. He burnt down my house. The fire trucks had to come and put the fire out. He had a gun and the police came down and got him so he burned my house down.

Q. Do you have any dreams of getting out of here?

L. Yeah. My dream is to get me a place and do some part time work or whatever. Have a place to stay with some hot water where you can take a shower whenever you want to. Turn the lights on, turn your TV on, you know? I haven't seen TV in about a year. I'd like to go to the movies. I'd like to have a woman. I'd like to have all these things everybody else has. What can a person really do in my situation? If I have to use the bathroom I have to go up to the hospital and use theirs. I wish I had running water.

ALEX L.

Alex is thirty-nine years old. He is a 5'9" white man who wears short pants and a turban which covers his almost waist length hair. He is very strong from skating and bike riding. At the time of this interview he had a knee high soft cast on his right leg from a bicycle accident.

Q. Alex, tell me how you survive. How do you get food?

A. Sometimes you get hungry enough to eat left-overs that people leave out on garbage cans, and what grocery stores throw out. I used to take all the bags out of the trash at In'n Out Burger and eat all the unopened catsup. There are feeding programs to go to. It's a white trash sort of association. They (the homeless) party (dope) their resources out and then they just end up like they were.

Q. Where do you sleep?

A. When I have to sleep I try to find boxes to put a roof over my head. I usually sleep in open parking lots because the space is not really accounted for like sleeping in someone's hedge. Sometimes you get tired enough to sleep wherever, wet and cold. I find boxes and bubble pack in dumpsters outside of stores and lay them down to sleep on. I had a really nice fleece jacket that I later got separated from.

Q. How do you get your clothes?

A. I first came to town with some nice clothes and skates, and I just skated around. Then someone took them and I felt like a bird, that just fell out of the nest. I find clothes everywhere. I get them from the backs of benches. I'll find a bag of clothes, maybe donations. I found a really nice leather jacket and a really nice long coat once. You don't touch other homeless people's things cause they might cause serious harm to you. There have been times I went to jail over this. People are really particular about their stuff. Some carry blades. A lot of people get out of prison. They don't have a lot of money. In a confrontation, the point is to get out WHOLE. You learn to have a killer attitude or you might have to run and leave your shit.

Q. What's your typical day?

A. I take catnaps around town all day. I stay up all night and sleep in the day when it's warm. Sometimes I sleep at the beach to get wet stuff dry. You watch out for drunk people and the like. They'll box you in. You have to keep an open space between you one side or the other to get away or for a better fighting position. I have been in situations where I've had to hustle my ass out. I had a comfortable childhood so people may think they have something on me but they don't. I know how things are supposed to be. There are a lot of trashy people out there.

Sometimes I sleep in doorways or in back of Churches. If I eat out of a trash can I eat the clean stuff on top. No egg or mayonnaise. Supermarkets throw away yogurt dated that day, or 20 cases of juice because it is dated. Sometimes it's real good eating. Sometimes the food is wet, the blankets are wet, your feet are wet.

Q. What are your hopes for the future?

A. My desire to be right isn't what it used to be. I have been receiving Social Security since 1996. Before that I was on General Relief. There have been days when I spent my money on—you know—stuff—'till I'm out of money, out of luck and coming down. The most important thing is to keep my morale high. When I'm down and out I start to feel ashamed, and this feeling is hard to conquer.

I suppose there are ways to get out of this trap and move up. If the person takes the hand-out one week, get shoes, the next month getting a suit and tie, then possibly they could be out selling cars. Then someone will say "Let's share the rent." This is possible.

Q. I know this is not easy. No resume, no transportation, licenses to pay for. Believe me, I know this is very difficult. What would you do to help a friend new on the street, like a girl who was out there for the first time?

A. I would help and protect her. I would always be there for her. Combat—keep your chin up and run away from an armed man. Run, turn a corner, run, turn another corner, run. If you don't haul ass it might be all over for you if he has a weapon. If your life is on the line, what the fuck do they matter? Know when you get bad vibes. Like a guy coming up to you to punch you. Some people you cannot turn your back on!

Losing something or misplacing something, fights can start like "I didn't take your shit" POW! The incentive to blame is the first smoke to go up. It makes you feel real bad if later you find it after accusing someone of stealing it.

I actually left this mental health center I was going to for about two months to see if I could survive on my own without it. I could. I love feeding the birds. I found this duck in the trash and I took it down to the pier to feed the seagulls. I threw it in the water, then I heard this sound, and a shark came up and had it in one gulp. I even heard its teeth go together.

Q. Any other survival tips?

A. Make sure you catch up on your sleep to stay strong. It's bad luck to share a storage locker. I've even stashed stuff in trees and bushes. Sometimes I buy bicycles from people. I don't want to know how the bike was acquired. One time I followed a guy to the Salvation Army dump box and pulled his skates out when nobody was around. I kind of live a stuntman life and I get lots of injuries.

ROBERT B.

Robert is a fifty-seven year old black man with some grey in his hair. He wears a baseball cap and is pushing a shopping cart half full of bottles and cans for recycling. Robert is going blind.

Q. Tell me something about yourself.

R. I was born in 1946 in Contra Costa. That's up north by San Francisco. They had an army base. So when my mother had me she was like seventeen. She couldn't deal with me, and then she gave me to some people when I was six weeks old. So they changed my name from Barber to Hicks. All through life I never knew that till I got ready to get married at the age of eighteen. Then I had to change my name back to Robert James Barber. Now I am fifty-seven years old. Hey, I used to work at Sunkist growers. Ok, I started off as a laborer. Then I became a mixer, and then a lead man. Then I had to go down in the tank. I slipped and I fell. I hurt my back. They put me into re-training, then they gave me my job back, then they laid me off after five years. When my mother and father died—black people they don't leave no Will—here come all the other relatives. They get everything. Now I'm out here trying to survive. I have been homeless since 1983. That's twenty years.

Q. Ever had any trouble with the law?

R. The only thing I've been arrested for—uh—when I was young, I went to YTS. I did six months. You see the parole people, then they get you out in three more months. And since then, nothing but traffic tickets.

Q. It looks like you're recycling now.

R. Right. Well, that's better than standing out begging. You can't find who's gonna give you something. So I go out and recycle. It's amazing what you might find.

Q. So, you get high once in awhile?

R. Uhh, I drink, but, hey, I can't afford that other shit (laughs). Like I tell people, one hit ain't enough and a thousand is too many. And I cannot afford it. But now, hey, I just left the liquor store, but all I did was buy a twenty-five cent cigarette.

Q. I'm sorry I didn't bring any smokes with me.

R. Hey, no sweat, hey, I don't beg. Sometimes I find me a butt, tear off the filter and keep on walking.

Q. Where do you sleep around these parts?

R. Any place that I can. Because, you know, ah, there might be one place that the police come and they may hassle you. So what you have to do is go from here to there, from here to there. Everybody knows me cause I always coming to the same spots.

Q. Do you get GR?

R. No, I don't. What I do I get food stamps. That's all I get here. I don't mess with them because GR is a hang up. It's a hassle. You're depending on them, you walk down there and then you don't have your shit. (Papers and proof of residency). If you figure it out they only giving you, if you add it up, that's less than seven dollars a day. Hey, you can get seven dollars, and go spend it and go about your business. I found me a little TV. (He shows me the TV in his cart.) Now, I got to get some batteries for this. And then what you have to do, you have to watch your stuff. Then you have to watch people, cause people will come who want to steal your stuff. (He picks up a broken steel baseball bat.) Now this is only for self preservation. Cause self preservation is the first law of life. I find me something, maybe I'll fix it up and somebody will buy it. Just keep your eyes open for things.

DONNA M.

Donna is a small lady about 5'4" with dark shoulder length hair, covered by the hood of a red sweat shirt. I found her at the park with her belongings around her. She also had a cage with two pet rats: one brown and the other white. She is forty-six years old.

Q. How did you first become homeless?

D. Divorce. My husband divorced me. But we're really not legally divorced. Nobody divorced anybody. I haven't seen him since the child was three years old. He'd be about 22 years old today. I couldn't pay the rent so I was living on the street ever since. During that time I worked about six years and nobody knew that I was homeless. I slept in my car. I had a day job, a swing shift job, and a graveyard shift job. And every now and then I would work in a bar as a waitress.

Q. How did you hurt your hand? (One hand was bandaged.)

D. I had surgery on my hand. The little finger was doing this number. (She showed me how stiff it was using her other hand). Harbor General took care of the operation. It is a County Facility so it was free. I've been on General Relief for years. I've had a broken hip, a broken knee so I keep getting medical extensions. My hip, I was trying to get out of the rain so I was running and I slipped on the pavement.

Q. How do you get food these days?

D. People just come. I hang out in the park and people keep dropping food off. I don't sleep in the park though. When it's not raining I sleep in an alley.

Q. Where do you get your clothes?

D. People give me more and more. I just don't have a place to put them all. I really don't travel very far because I have to be careful my stuff's not lost. The park rangers tag your stuff, and if you're not there in an hour, they haul it away.

Q. Do you ever go to the shelter?

D. Well, you have to be in at 5:45 PM and I just can't deal with their curfew. I usually bed down around 7:00 at night. There are the night crawlers. (She motions to where people are sleeping.) Sleep all day and then up all night. They party, they smoke shit. At night I like to be asleep. In the day you hear the trash trucks, the delivery trucks.

Q. Do you see your way out of this?

D. No, not right now, unless I was willing to go into a shelter which I am not ready to do. In the shelter they keep some of your check and hold it. They kick you out in the morning, and I just am not going to do this. They have like cots. They give you jobs like chores but they don't pay you. Sweep the floor, clean the bathroom, do the laundry, dust the bookshelves. Not to mention, I have my rats. (She opens the top of the cage and pets the brown rat. I left at this point.)

DON O.

It was 6:30 A.M. in downtown Santa Monica. The homeless were wearily walking away from where they slept the night before. I had gone out early for a pack of cigarettes and I met Don, who was also out for cigarettes. Only he was searching for them on the sidewalk.

Don is a six foot, man size guy, with newly-cut red/blond hair under his baseball cap. He is forty-six years old.

Q. Where are you from initially, Don?

D. Ohio.

Q. How long have you been homeless?

D. A good five years. I've been out here seven months in Los Angeles. I'd come out here to Santa Monica in the summertime, and I'd get in trouble. So I stay up and down the coast.

Q. What do you do for food?

D. I panhandle, ask people for food. Here in Santa Monica is one of the best places to be. Santa Monica and Venice. These days I'm sleeping over there next to the library.

Q. What time do you get to sleep around here?

D. It varies, like last night I was probably out before 8:00 o'clock. This morning I was out looking for a place to use the bathroom. I said, "I'm not gonna take a dump in the alley". I went to Vons. They were all out of tokens there so I got a quarter from the cash register. I opened the door and, looking in there, damn, there was a pile of toilet paper in the toilet up to the brim. There was no way I could use it, so I went back to get another quarter. Everyone was using the women's bathroom and it was open, so I got a quarter out of it.

Q. How do you stay clean?

D. I go to the Swash lock at the Salvation Army. It's pretty cool cause they'll bring you food once in a while there. They got shaving cream, shampoo, underarm deodorant. They'll wash your clothes, and if you need a pair of socks or a shirt they might have one for you. On the first of the month I get drunk on other people's money and then I got to pay them back.

Q. Did you have any conflicts out here on the street?

D. As a matter of fact I had a dream about it last night. I was in this nightclub and I got something stuck in my brain. My brother was in it. We almost got into a fight. I had been up. I had very little sleep in the last four days cause I just got out of jail. I was in jail for some cocaine. I spent twenty-six nights. I got out of jail on a drug diversion program. So I'm starting it up on the 8th. Anyway, about this fight, you know I was getting drunk on Saturday night and I had been partying since Friday night. I was real drunk and pretty tired. I was near the pier and this one guy said to another guy that he was wondering where he was. There was aggravation and this one guy came at me and I had to sidestep him. I had to put down my bag. I was too tired and he would have knocked me down. So I had seen him before down at the Red Roses in Venice, which is a good place to eat and get hooked up with St. Joseph's. You make reservations a day ahead of time. We'd sit there and they would come out and serve you with plates. I got my mailing address there.

Q. Do you have any dreams of getting out of this?

D. You know what? Now that I'm older as far as to come up with a good dream, well I just try to go with the flow. When I get rest it's easier for me to dream. It's hard to get a good night's rest. Of course I'd rather be on a bed. The situation is that it's always a struggle. But there are lots of places to eat. I was going to get into that Salvation Army shelter there. Say, can I get a couple of cigarettes?

(I gave him some cigarettes. It seems like there's little way for Don to get off the train he's on.)

TOM H.

Tom is a white male with short brown hair. He's about 5'9" and is thirty-nine years old. He's from the South Eastern U.S. and has a pleasing personality. I interviewed him at Step-Up on Second.

Q. Tell me when you became homeless and how you survived.

T. I graduated high school in '83. I first became homeless in 1996. I was in Virginia—Norfolk, Virginia, and I didn't like the weather. I panhandled money, and I kept saving money and I bought me a ticket to California—to Los Angeles.

I was living in the streets of Los Angeles and then, when my money ran out I would panhandle. I had this certain corner on sixth street in downtown L.A. that I would panhandle and make three, four, five bucks a day. I ate off of that and bought coffee and cigarettes. I was about two blocks away from skid row. I ended up there eventually. But I didn't like it because of the atmosphere. You see women with kids and dope. You know I seen people smokin' you know pot, you know, crack, and all the beer, and just finally one day you know, one day I just got on the bus and came to Santa Monica. It was just two bucks. Because everyone was smokin' drugs you know, drinkin' and, you know, fighting and, you know, I just didn't want to be around that atmosphere.

I slept in an alley. I had a couple of covers, blankets. I would put the cardboard down on the concrete and I'd sleep with cardboard over me. I couldn't find no place to shower to get cleaned up. I was filthy. I was in Skid row about a month and a week before I found Santa Monica. And I was sittin' on the bus stop one day, you know, and there was this black boy. I can still remember today. He walked up and asked me if I had any change. You know, I mean this kid was filthy. So I had like a couple bucks in change and I saved enough to get on the bus and then I gave him the rest. He wadn't I'd say no more than thirteen or fourteen I guess, and he was living on the street. But he told me what bus to get on. He sat there so I got on the bus that would come to Santa Monica. And if I had more money I would have gave it to him but that's all the money I had.

When I got off the bus I was nervous, like I was when I was downtown, but I could feel the atmosphere. It wasn't as dangerous in Santa Monica as it was in downtown skid row. I got here in Santa Monica in January of 1999 and I'm still homeless.

I've survived by panhandling, and, do you know what dumpster diving is? Going through the dumpster, you know. When I was sleeping on skid row you have to sleep with one eye open and the other eye closed cause, you know, cause you have all the gangs and drugs and violence around. I like the weather and the atmosphere and the people in Santa Monica. I'm afraid to go down town by myself anymore, you know. I won't go downtown cause, you know, I've been around that atmosphere. I've been around drugs, I been around the alcohol. I see people doing that and I don't want to be involved in it so I just stay around here.

Q. What is your panhandling technique?

T. You know I wouldn't hold a sign, you know. I just rattle my cup. The only time I'd say somethin' is "thank you" when they put money in my cup.

Q. What is your typical day?

T. On some days I come here (Step-Up on Second) and see my doctor. I pick up my meds here and get my meals. I attend about three groups a week. I found all my clothes dumpster diving. If I saw somebody who was about to throw something out, and it was cleaner than my clothes, I would ask them for it. I first got on SSI in 2000. Before that I was on GR and food stamps.

Q. Did you have any Police trouble?

T. Yeah. Nothin' serious, you know. They'd come up, you know, when you're sleeping and shine the light in your eyes and ask you for an I.D. And they'd run you, you know, for warrants you know. But other than that, no. I've had like a couple of jay walking tickets that turned into warrants and they picked me up, you know, and I'd spend one night in jail, you know. Went to court and the Judge said, "time served." I usually hang by myself, you know. Sleep on the street by myself. That way I don't get into trouble. Now I've been sleeping in a vacant building.

Q. What about your medical care?

T. I've had to see a medical doctor once in awhile. Medi-Cal pays for that. I cut myself once and had to go and get it taken care of in the emergency room you know. That was about the only major thing.

Q. Any plans for the future?

T. I don't think I'm able to work now you know, according to my doctor. I don't want to stay homeless all my life. The reason why you got a lot of homeless people out here being homeless is there ain't enough affordable housing for everybody. Lots of them gets income like me. There just ain't enough affordable housing to go around.

I could maybe get myself a part time job. Make a couple extra bucks during the week. I had a stipend job here for awhile but I was afraid that Social Security was going to say something so I quit. I'm not getting younger, you know, and there will come a time when I'll have to be housed. Being on the street isn't all that healthy for you, you know.

MICHELLE C.

Michelle is a small Caucasian woman of fifty-two. She looks older, but that's the age she gave me. She was wearing large sunglasses when I interviewed her at the park.

Q. When did you first become homeless?

M. About two months ago. I lost my job and I couldn't pay my rent. It was such a traumatic experience. It's really been the worst thing I've been through in my entire life. So what happened was that I didn't have the money to pay the rent and I was evicted. I ended up selling all my possessions, my furniture and personal effects, TV and some of my clothes. That money I could use to live on for a while. And so I just kept my car, and I've been living in my car for the past two months.

I'm fifty-two and I wasn't expecting to have to go through all this. And, ah, so it's been pretty tough trying to find another job. Because it's hard for people to contact me. I don't have a residence. I don't have a phone. I don't know how people who don't have cars to live in survive. My biggest fear is, if I don't find a job before the money runs out, I'll have to sell my car, you know, so I can have that money to live on. And then living on the street—it's the most terrifying thing. I just don't know how people do it.

Q. What kind of work were you doing?

M. Well, what I was doing was, um, customer service, working for a Telecommunications Company. One of these companies that, um, provides adult fantasy and telephone physic services to people. My job was to take the information from the customers that would call that were requesting these services. Like, I'd have to check the credit card number and process payments and things like that. And, do some selling. They would call and ask for information about the services, what the prices were for, like, a ten or twenty minute call. I'd give that information to them. That's basically what my job was.

I was in that job for twelve years. The company just wasn't making enough money and I got laid off. They closed their doors and laid everyone off. It was just a big shock. I wasn't expecting it. I thought that things were going ok. I thought "Oh God, what am I going to do?" At night I park in a residential area when I sleep.

Q. What do you do for food?

M. I try to stretch my money as far as I can. I do a lot of shopping at the 99 Cent Store. I can get a bag of eight English muffins for 99 cents and I have one of those for breakfast every day. So that's like a week's breakfast. Then for lunch sometime, I'll buy like some tuna fish. They are two for 99 cents. Or, sometimes three for ninety-nine cents. I try and get as much as I can for my money and make it stretch—make it last for a few days. I have gotten a few meals down here at the park. I've been going there whenever it's been available.

Q. Do you ever panhandle?

M. No, I don't know. I just don't feel like I have the guts to do that. (laughs) I find a couple of ways to make a few dollars here and there, like I've been collecting bottles and cans so I make a few dollars that way. I know of some resale shops like in the Hollywood area where I've been taking a few of my clothes.

I spend a lot of my time in the library. I go through every newspaper that I can, looking at the want ads for some place where they wouldn't have to call me because I don't have a phone—someone who I could talk to in person where I could explain my situation. I'm trying to do positive things, like being around places that offers opportunities. Sometimes I just go to the pier and sit there, or read. I try to think things through as much as I can and try not to worry about what I'm going to do. Like where I'm going to get food. The evenings are the worst part because I hate sleeping in my car. But so far no one's bothered me. I should go to the dentist because I'm a little worried about my teeth. If I get a job that would really fix me up. I would be able to replace those things that I lost. The most important thing is getting a job.

CLIFF J.

Cliff is a fifty-seven year old Caucasian male of average height. He has long graying hair and a small moustache. He is very tanned and has a couple of tattoos on his arms and legs.

Q. Cliff, how did you happen to become homeless?

C. Alcohol, drinking on the job. I was married for a long time and was m adly in love with my ex. Still am. The relationship degenerated because of alcohol and drugs. I was drinking at lunch time and before I went to work.

Q. What kind of childhood did you have?

C. I had a devastating childhood. My father was a police officer in Philadelphia. He beat me unceasingly. When I was four he kidnapped me and my sister from my mother, and it took her a year to find us, and she kidnapped us back. This was in 1950.

Q. How has being homeless affected you?

C. When I first became homeless it really didn't bother me. I'm city-wise and country-bred. I know how to make it anywhere. I've traveled the country. Fought forest fires with the U.S. Forest Service. Slept in the gravel of creek beds, so sleeping out really doesn't bother me. These days I have a girl friend and we have a really good spot behind a building. The owner knows we're there. I have a little pop-up tent. We've been there about three months. We keep it clean back there.

Q. Where do you get food?

C. I do a re-cycling run every day. On a daily basis we've made about twenty-five bucks a day. People on my route give me clothes. I have a lot of medical problems, which is why I came out here. Most of my medical records are here. Technically, I am somewhat disabled, and do qualify for GR. I don't panhandle, but I sure know how to. I don't want to bother people.

Q. Tell me what a typical day is like for you.

C. On my route we're up at 5:30 in the morning and usually done by 8:30. At 8:45 I'll drink a forty ounce beer. Then we'll have breakfast. Then grab the bus into town to check and see if we have any mail, or to keep appointments like doctors, or counseling appointments. If not, well, it's just another beautiful day in California. I'll go to the park, put the tarp down on the grass and read. I love to read. We don't have a big agenda.

Q. Have you run into any trouble?

C. I have had a little trouble out here. I had to put someone in jail. I'm a certified Minister and give counseling sometimes. I had been counseling this guy for quite awhile over the loss of his girlfriend. I had been talking to him a bit, and he wouldn't stop crying and whining. He wouldn't stop. Two weeks ago he came over drunk and started in again. I told him I didn't want to hear it. I went to the park office and told them to call 911 because there's going to be trouble. Just then he pushed my woman. Next thing I knew we were throwing ching gossos, man. The fight was on. The police came—three cops and the fire department, and they hauled his ass off to jail.

Q. You mentioned you were somewhat disabled. In what way?

C. I have a whole lot of physical problems. I have a left knee that is hyperextended. They told me to come back in about fifteen years for a replacement. I need a carpal-tunnel operation on my right wrist. I've already had one done on my left. I've got a slight case of Elephant man's disease. Have you ever seen the movie? I've got lumps and bumps in my chest. My biggest worries are dental problems. They told me I need four thousand five hundred dollars worth of dental work, out of pocket.

Q. Do you have any plans for the future?

C. I lived in Hawaii for two years on a sailboat, and I'd like to go to Tahiti. I like to work with wood. I do porches and deck remodeling. That's the kind of work I do. Landscaping, sprinklers, lighting, etc. I've done all that kind of stuff. If I had to do it all over again—I can see how drinking ruined my success. In the sixties it was drugs, sex and rock and roll. I've worked in the tittie bars and all that. I've DJ'd in Tittie bars. I even miss all that! My ex wives are married to people, and they have homes and cars and go on vacations. But they still have their own problems with the mortgages and car payments. It doesn't matter who you are. If you've got a million dollars you have a million dollar's worth of problems. But I'd rather have money and problems than no money and problems.

BURN B.

Burn is a forty-five year old Caucasian male. He is about five feet, six inches tall and has almost shoulder length blond hair. He is well tanned.

Q. How long have you been homeless?

B. I became homeless about a month ago. I worked for Disney and I worked for Fox Family channel about three and a half years. Then Disney bought our company and laid off everyone. They just wanted to buy the contracts. I got laid off. Then I lost my apartment and my dad died. A lot of things happened. I started doing drugs.

Previously my two sisters committed suicide and when I was two my mom died in police custody. When I first became homeless I was scared. I was terrified.

Q. How do you get food?

B. I get food from food lines. (He showed me a typed-up piece of paper with about thirty places to go where they serve meals.) Sometimes you hear of stuff that isn't on the list. You can get them at various feeding places. (He points to one on the list.) This one I don't attend because they ram the Bible up your ass.

Q. Where do you usually sleep?

B. Now I'm sleeping in an alley. I sleep with two blankets and I sleep on a piece of cardboard. I sleep with my I.D. and stuff. I figure some day I'll lose that. Someone's going to rob me. The only clothes I have are the ones I have on except a couple of T-shirts that are in the laundry now. There's this establishment I know that has showers and laundry machines for the homeless.

Q. Do you panhandle?

B. No. I get GR. Sometimes I do these focus groups. You watch their television programs or commercials and they pay you twenty to fifty, sometimes a hundred dollars for your input of their questions. What you like, didn't like and other input. There's a smoking research I'm going to be in that will probably pay me good money. I have a list of these places and I call around and make money that way.

Q. What's a typical day for you?

B. I go get breakfast where they feed people. Then I go to the park and read. In the evenings I go to the alley with my friends, 'cause there's safety in numbers. The blacks run around robbing people at night. Especially now. They've run out of their GR 'cause they smoked it up in a pipe and there went your GR.

Q. What are your biggest worries?

B. Closing my eyes at night. There was another time that I was homeless in 1997. I had a crack habit which got me evicted. I stayed homeless for about a year.

You have to look around for a certain type of people who are safe to be around, and that's your safety net.

Q. What are your dreams for the future?

B. I have no dreams. I have nothing. I don't know what I want. I'm just doing this day by day.

JOHN M.

John is about 5'10", a Caucasian male with black hair, and needs a haircut. He is thirty-eight years old.

Q. When did you initially become homeless?

J. When I was seventeen years old. The parents kicked me out. It was pouring down rain. I eventually got jobs, going from one to the next. I was housed a few times in between. When I was doing private estate management I usually had my home on the estate. I was taking care of people's personal property. I was managing their small businesses, like signing for packages, picking up deliveries and doing the shopping. The people owned acres that had to be maintained. I worked for two different families.

The money was pretty good. Mental illness hadn't set in yet. Mental illness didn't set in 'till about '89 or '90. My first symptoms were bouts of serious depression. Jobs started to fall apart. Relationships started to fall apart. Basically taking care of my self became a problem. I had extreme ups and extreme downs. I was diagnosed with bipolar and major depression.

Q. Let's go back a few years. How did you do in school?

J. I did pretty well in school. I was raised in South Central Los Angeles. I dropped out of High school, and went to continuation school. At the same time I was going for my certified nurse certification. I ended up doing private care.

Q. How were your parents?

J. My mom is a very vicious person. There was a lot of physical and mental abuse. It wasn't a very happy childhood to say the least. Nothing I did was good enough for her.

Q. How are you surviving now?

J. I get SSI. Basically, when I get my money at the beginning of the month and manage it, I take care of my basic necessities. If the money runs out, I go to the food lines. Sometimes I dig out of the garbage can. Or, sometimes where I sleep, somebody will walk by and hand me something they have like leftovers or something like that.

Q. Where do you sleep?

J. I sleep in a doorway. It's a safe doorway, so long as I'm out by 6:00 A.M. I have a really nice army sleeping bag. I carry my stuff with me wherever I go. I really don't trust anybody.

Q. When is the last time you worked?

J. My last job ended last January. I was doing live-in support for a terminal HIV case. We had to place him in a Hospice care facility. Eventually he passed away.

Q. Do you panhandle?

J. I have panhandled. It's something I really hate to do.

Q. What's a typical day for you?

J. A typical day for me is going to a care center attending a couple of group meetings—self help groups. I shower and wash my clothes if I can. I talk to my case manager, talk to friends that I know.

Q. What are the nights like?

J. I've had to sleep with one eye open a lot. I think the biggest fear of sleeping on the streets is, for instance, one night I got this feeling that someone was standing over me. I woke up, and sure enough someone was standing over me. Another biggest fear is hate crimes. There are, in fact, people who hate the homeless. There have been several attacks on the homeless you know.

Q. Do you get any medical attention?

J. I do go see my Psychiatrist. I have been in the hospital for ten day stays because of my illness, to get re-adjusted to new medications and what not.

My hopes have been to really get the pieces of my life back together. My ultimate dream is to eventually get my Vocational Nursing license. I want to go back to work and make a decent living. In San Francisco there is a program for people on SSI that can go back to work, and earn extra money and acquire a license like a Vocational Nurse.

Q. What would you have done differently in your life?

J. If I had the choice, I would have chosen different parents.

MELINDA W.

Melinda is a Caucasian lady with straight blond hair past her shoulders. She stands about five foot two inches and is forty-six years old. She appears to be much younger.

M. I have been homeless about three years or four years all together. I'm from Indiana. I came here with my boyfriend. We've been together four years, and he's a welder. He came out here to do a job for Anheuser-Busch. He has a bad back now and he applied for SSDI and he could no longer weld and that's the only trade he's ever done. So now he's got his SSDI and he don't have to work. So I'm with my boyfriend and we're both homeless.

Q. How do you feel about being homeless?

M. Being homeless at first was scary. You know, the idea of being out on the streets, not having the things for your basic needs. When we first became homeless we were in the Valley, and then we stayed in downtown L.A. And my boyfriend got money for about six months retro-active. Then I found out about GR which I didn't know anything about. In California they have a lot of means, a lot of help for the homeless.

GR is a check and food stamps every month that they give the homeless people. You get like $221.00 on your check and right now I get $139.00 on my stamps. We were in downtown L.A. for six or seven. And then we came here and we found out about St. Joseph's. It's a good program. You go into case management and they have Swashlock, which is showers, lockers and laundry. And you can get bus tokens and anything you need like clothing and hygiene. It makes it easier to be homeless. There are other places to get clothing also. You have a Family Clinic and there's St. John's Hospital. It's all free to the homeless. Your needs get met here. There's a spot where we sleep in a vacant lot, unless we get our money and go to a motel for about a week. It's just us two and there's no one else back there. You know, it's a good spot. We've never had any problem sleeping back there. I usually use the restrooms in fast food places.

Q. Do you earn any extra money?

M. Like, sometimes they do surveys on the mall, you can do something like that. I used to panhandle. I worked the promenade for about five of six months. If I didn't have something else to do I would go there and panhandle.

Q. What's a typical day for you?

M. I go to Swashlock every day. I go there twice a day. Um, if I have a doctor's appointment or other appointments or case management, I'll do that. I eat at food lines. Every day varies a little.

Q. Did you two have to protect yourselves at any time?

M. We were in downtown L.A. one time and my boy friend got into an argument with someone. It was a black guy, and I'm not prejudiced or anything, but the guy did pull a knife on him. So my boyfriend just talked to him and the guy backed off. That was the only time. I think the guy was trying to rob us. We didn't have any money. I've been diagnosed with schizophrenia and depression.

Q. What advice would you give to someone who just became homeless?

M. Uhm, just check things out and find out about everything that's available. Things like GR, medical. You can even get your mail at St. Joseph's, messages, case management. There may be a shelter, too.

C.L.

C.L. is a small Caucasian man with a sharp, just over the ears, haircut. He has brown hair and is almost thirty-four years old. He looks harmless. He prefers to just give his initials rather than his name.

Q. When and why did you become homeless?

C. I first became homeless from the sex, drugs and rock an' roll. I thought I was going to do a lot without working, although I did work some jobs from time to time. This was in 1987, just after my first major incarceration. I had a standoff with the police in Portland, Oregon. I had a thirty aught six rifle. I got about a year for that. They had put me in the Oregon State Hospital.

I'd have to say that my story is a sad story, but I had a lot of fun. My father was kind of strict. He didn't really beat me all that much, but he did once or twice. When I first became homeless it didn't even affect me. I was a drummer, and like I said, I was just numb. Even in the freezing cold of the Pacific Northwest. I was stoned out of my mind half the time. There were some times when I was sober, and regretting that biting freeze, that icy stormy cross. That's where I was in 1987 and 1988. Since then I've been in jail about forty or fifty times at least.

Q. What charges have been brought against you?

C. In the 90's, theft, a lot of assaults, like strong arm robbery. That did happen once. It was dropped to a second degree commercial burglary. Maybe ten or twelve were serious incarcerations.

Q. Did you ever have to go to a doctor or hospital?

C. A black person put some medication in my beer once. I don't know if he was just trying to be cool or what. That put me in the hospital.

Q. Tell me some more about your past.

C. When I was young I would visit my biological father and his other sons, my brothers through two other women. I grew up with my sister from my stepfather, but now I hardly write and she hardly writes me anymore. I've been in prison a lot. I'm still a musician though, but not really. I'm out of practice.

Q. How did you do in school?

C. I did terrible in school. I thought I was a lot more intellectual than they did. Obviously I wanted to go out and live, explore. So I'd skip school frequently. I'd have good attendance and then go off on a little binge, you know, a nature hike you know. That's the way that went.

Q. What's a typical day for you?

Q. These days I hang out with a lot of homeless, especially when it comes time to eat. I go to the food lines. I've been sleeping on the beach the last few years. It's gone now. They just built a huge house on it. Then I got locked up again. Now I'm sleeping in the bushes behind palm trees adjacent to that property. Those cops are going to be the death of me. I hope they don't find me where I'm sleeping.

Q. What do you do about clothes?

C. Somehow I got my clothes washed the other day. Irish Spring seemed to work. I worked for some of these clothes in prison. Some of them are stolen.

Q. Are you getting GR?

C. No. I applied and that was a one time thing. I got some food stamps one time. I was pretty much forced back on the streets by the parole agencies. My last case, it was self defense, they locked me up anyway. They've really got me on the run.

Q. How do you get money?

C. I don't panhandle. I don't want to bother anybody. They usually just hand me money.

Q. What's your biggest worry?

C. Living day by day. The female tends to change my whole outlook sometimes. But they can really be fucked up too. Having a girl friend makes me want to live. It's just another obsession, another addiction. I'm not getting any, but it's something I tend to live for. I still have dreams of being a musician. I been working on that but it just isn't happening. The way things have worked out, I feel kind of fortunate. I wouldn't have done anything different. I enjoy the good, and I just have to go through the bad.

KEN K.

I met Ken in the park. He is a tall Caucasian man with blond, crew cut hair. He is thirty-one years old, and has two tattoos on each arm and on both legs.

Q. When did you become homeless, Ken?

K. Well it usually starts when everything is going good, and then it all falls apart. I've gone in with people on places before and usually it goes good until they wind up just flaking out. Not wanting to pay their share of the bills, and I wouldn't be able to pay it all so I'd lose my place to live.

Q. Are you working at all now?

K. I push carts on the Promenade. It's a little bit of money. Two other guys I know are homeless also, and it's like we are trying to save up. Get a place, and not have to worry about "Oh, okay, if I go to sleep here in the park and I decide I want to cover up, am I going to get a ticket? Am I going to get rousted by the cops?" A lot of people that are on the streets like in the newspaper, they say are drug addicts and all that. Well, more of them are like mentally ill. Some, yeah, they like to drink. Myself, I'm like bipolar and I suffer from a social anxiety disorder. I take medication and it just keeps me mellow. But 95% of the people on the streets are mentally ill. It's like they don't know what to do. It's like their families say "come home" and they go home for maybe a couple of days to a week, and they don't know what to do, and they wind up back here.

Myself, it's like I try to not look homeless. It's like with the money I make from pushing carts I'll like go out and buy myself nice clothes. Got a cell phone so if they need to get in touch with me. Make no bones about it, I tell people I'm homeless, but I try to make my appearance look like I'm not, because I don't want to be discriminated against.

When it would rain, we wouldn't work. So I went to Barnes and Noble with my big backpack on. They'd start following me around thinking I'm going to steal. And it's like I'd have money in my pocket, I'm like "Look, I'm buying this magazine." They'd say, "Oh no no no, you stole something in your bag." I'm like, "You know what, check it, and when you don't find anything you best be prepared to hear from a lawyer. I don't care how I'm gonna do it, but I'm gonna get a lawyer and sue you for discrimination." I don't know how much I've got saved up, but I've got a nice little chunk, and I figure by the end of the summer I'll hopefully be indoors.

Q. Where did you live before you came here?

K. I grew up in New Jersey, and it's like whatever school I was at, me and my dad would always get in a fight. He's like "you're going to work this summer."

I'm like, "No, I'm not." I would run away. I would either go to New York City, or I'd hop on a Greyhound and come out here to California. I first started coming to Santa Monica when I was fourteen. Long before the Promenade was ever thought of. I was hanging out on the beach by the pier. I didn't look fourteen so I could usually pass anywhere eighteen to twenty. I wouldn't tell people my age because they'd think they could get over on me.

In 1989 I went into the service. Was in from '89 to '95. I had a place to live up until let's say a couple days before I came back out here in April of '96, because my lease was up. I wound up losing my job. So I bought a bus ticket and came out here. Came out thinking that I was going to be working at a club, bouncing. My uncle set it up for me, but it never happened. So I wound up homeless.

Q. What did you do to survive?

K. I had to sell drugs or whatever to make ends meet to get a hotel room, or to save up to get an apartment. I tattooed people in Hollywood. I was probably one of the biggest drug dealers, and that's something I really wasn't proud of. Let alone selling it, I was using. Wound up coming back here in I'd say June of '96, got fed up with Hollywood and decided I wanted to be by the beach. Got mixed up in the drug thing again. Went back to Hollywood, in a squat that me and my friends were staying in. Someone went in there and stole all our stuff. The only pictures I had of my youngest son. It was like, that was my life in there. So I had a bunch of cocaine, a bunch of speed, mixed it all together, chopped it up, made really big fat lines, and tried to kill myself.

Q. Obviously, you didn't succeed. What did you do then?

K. Uh, I went into a rehab program March 10th of '97, and I stayed clean until about three weeks till I came back here in 2001. And it was like an on again, off again thing. I know how to control my drug habit now. If I want to snort a couple lines of coke, snort a couple lines of speed, but I made the decision not to go mad. I don't like doing it, but when you're homeless, stuff's offered, it helps you forget the situation you're in. But I can be grateful that I've got a job pushing carts. It's not much, but it's something.

Q. Tell me more about your childhood.

K. Well, I was born in Germany, raised in Nebraska and New Jersey with my biological mother and father. I was about three when we came from Germany in '74. My step-dad was in the Military. He uprooted us, took me away from all my friends that I had known since I was yea big (He brings his hand about three feet off the ground.) and moved me to New Jersey. I didn't fit in there. It's like I'm a little mid-western kid, and everyone started making fun of me. Got turned onto cocaine because I wanted to be like my uncle. He had a bad coke habit. So, I would see him doing the stuff, and when he left for a while, I would try the stuff.

I had a nervous breakdown shortly thereafter, and wound up being committed for a year in a children's psychiatric unit because I set my mom and dad's house on fire. My mom, my dad and his sisters were like, "Why did you do this? Are you stupid?" They didn't have a really good childhood. Her dad was very abusive to her and my grandma. My step-dad believed in corporal punishment when I was younger. It was like, "Okay, drop your pants. Face the corner." Whack, whack, whack!

I took it 'till I was thirteen when I finally stood up to the man. I had been studying martial arts. It took that for him to realize, you know what, it ain't gonna happen no more. There were some rough times. I harbored a lot of resentment. My mom—I would have had a twin sister, but my real dad pushed my mom down the stairs when she was eight months pregnant, and my sister was stillborn. Whenever my mom would get mad at me she would say, "You know, I wished your sister would have survived and you wouldn't have."

Q. What is your life like now? Are you eating okay?

K. The little bit of money I make pushing the carts I'm able to get a bite to eat in the mall or the Food Court around the Promenade. Or, ask people on the Promenade if they want their leftovers. There was one time in the summer of 2001 where I had been up for about a week and a half straight, doing so much speed. Well, I didn't have money to get something to eat, but I had all this money for the person I was selling drugs for. Do I use it to eat? Or, do I just give it to him? So I said, fuck it, I'm making him thousands of bucks, I'm going to get a five dollar value meal at McDonald's. So you do what you gotta do to survive.

When I moved back here in 2001 I had a car and everything. Took a couple of people down to San Ysidro. One of them wanted to go to Tijuana. He'd never been there. The other would buy cigarettes at the duty-free store. We'd cross over and come back.

One night they decided they wanted to get laid. So they invited this chick that had just gotten out of jail back to the room. Everything that I worked for, for three and a half years was gone in an instant. The girl they wanted to have sex with, that didn't even sleep with them, wanted to have sex with me but I wouldn't. I guess she found my car keys, took the car and all my clothes. My mountain bike that I spent $3000.00 on was in the back. Gone in the blink of an eye. I was violated.

I ran out to the front of the motel and got on the phone and called 911. They said is this an emergency? I said like, yeah, my car was just stolen from outside of this motel. They said, that's not an emergency. You need to call dispatch. I said, I need a sheriff here right now! This happened in San Ysidro. San Diego county sheriffs didn't do anything.

I went down to the Greyhound bus center. There was a couple of sheriffs there. I explained what happened. They said, "We don't have time." I called the California Highway Patrol. I gave them all the information on my car. They were the only ones that made an attempt to find it. Now it's either in a chop shop or it's in Mexico somewhere being used as a cop car or taxi in Tijuana.

When I was coming back up here I had a little pet rat—the most lovable little critter. Had him in his holder, which I then put in a pillow case to get on the Greyhound bus. That's the only thing I had left that meant anything to me. They told me that I couldn't get on the bus with my rat. So I went and found this American couple down in San Diego, sight-seeing. I had him on my shoulder. I walked up and said, "Excuse me" to this lady, "what do you think of my rat?" She said, "Oh, he's adorable. Where did you get him?" They were out of Santa Monica. I said, "Guess what, it's your lucky day. They won't let me ride the bus with him." I told them my car had just been stolen. I gave it to them. I said, "His name is Badger, take care of him."

All I had was the clothes on my back. I was in those clothes for two friggin weeks. I was desperate. I called my mom up. I was in tears, cause I had never been violated like that before. She winded up sending me a little bit of money. I went out and bought some clothes. Some people I knew started giving me stuff. Now I try and return the favor to other homeless people.

Q. Where do you sleep here, Ken?

K. These days I sleep in a parking lot. We have permission to be there from the owner, which is really, really cool.

Q. Do you get any GR or SSI?

K. I don't get either. I could apply for SSI but, you know what? The way I look at it, when it comes down to it, and I find that I can't work no more, then I'm going to apply for it. GR, when I tried to apply for it, they shot me down. So, I do a hustle here, a hustle there.

These days I'm up between 7:00 and 8:15 A.M., go drop off my stuff in the garage where we push the carts. I make the coffee on the coffee cart, fill others up with ice. I push the carts to their proper places from 9:30 to 11:30. There are seven carts including one food cart. Then I usually take a shower after that. There's a place where I have permission to use the shower. If I didn't sleep real good the night before, I will get a little to eat, then go up to the park and sleep like three or four more hours. At night I push the carts back, and I'm done.

Q. Have you ever had to protect yourself on the street?

K. Oh yeah! I haven't been in a fight since the day I got sober in '97. I won that fight. People are intimidated from my size and my tattoos, but I'm probably one of the nicest guys anyone will ever meet.

My youngest son is a mom's boy. She left me for another guy. The guy she left me for, I let him move into the apartment with me in Hollywood. We made amends 'cause she did him wrong like she did me. I was clean from drugs at the time. He starts doing crack cocaine, speed, heroin. I would notice stuff missing now and then. I ended up kicking him out, but not before he stole my driver's license information. He got a ticket for something.

This cop I knew said, "Ken, I got to arrest you for a ticket from 1998." I'm like okay, whatever. I was in jail for three and a half hours. He brought the ticket in before I went to court. We compared the signature from my driver's license and they didn't match. So I did time served and I let it go at that. I've only been arrested twice. I should have been arrested a lot of times for selling speed out here. I'm just grateful that I never got caught. I tell people who are doing that now that just because I never got caught, don't you do it, don't be stupid.

I was in a psychiatric hospital before I went into the service. Back in January I went to see my doctor, and I told him I was losing it. I need to go to a hospital for a seventy-two hour hold. He said no way. I went back to work, got my paxil. It didn't help me because my nerves were gone. I thought I was having another nervous breakdown. I don't like the way some of my friends treat me like a bum. But a bum refuses to work. They beg for money. I don't. I'm homeless, but I'm working class. The job takes a lot out of me but I'm earning my money every day.

Q. What do you dream you'd like to be doing?

K. I want to find a nice place in another city or another state where no one knows me. Where I'm able to start off with a clean slate. I would work myself up, start off in a small apartment and work my way up to a nice big house, settle down and raise a family.

I spoke to this girl that a friend of mine set me up with for ninety minutes on the phone. She's gonna come down and we're gonna meet up here and maybe go down to Venice. We'll probably sit down and have a couple of drinks and a nice lunch. Because if she's the girl I think she is, this is the girl I want to settle down with. If it happens it happens, if it doesn't it doesn't.

Q. What would you have done differently in your life?

K. Well, instead of enlisting in the Military like I did. I was accepted into the Naval Academy, I was accepted into the Air force Academy in Colorado. I had the opportunity to play football and hockey for some schools. I should have done that instead of enlisting and paying my way through college.

I graduated college in three and a half years. Bachelor of Science and Political Science. Bachelor of Science and Criminal Justice. I wouldn't have been disillusioned by the Marines as much. I was Military Police and also Special Forces. I would have made a career out of it. I would have winded up being in Officer's Candidate school. I wish I had gone through the Academy because I would have had a better life right now. I'd probably be married, have kids running around. But now I'm out here trying to make it as best I can.

JOHN D.

John is a tall Caucasian male with crew cut dark hair, and a sun tan. He is a gentle, soft spoken southern Florida man. He is forty-five years old.

Q. How are you today, John?

J. Well, my self esteem level is pretty low today. Actually my situation now—I want to get back to St. Petersburg. After working in St. Pete I drew all my unemployment out, had a few hundred dollars. I said I'm gonna go to southern California, find a place and start fresh. But with no local references, not knowing anybody, it was a foolish thing. So I want to get back. This may sound off the wall, but there's a truck stop in Riverside on Interstate 10 and maybe I can get lucky and hook up with a trucker and help him load and unload in exchange for a ride. I've been homeless a few months.

Q. Tell me something about your childhood.

J. I had a pretty good childhood. I liked baseball. A normal childhood I would say—a pretty loving family.

Q. What was your last employment?

J. A caretaker. I took care of a couple. I assisted them, drove them. I lived on the premises in a little garage apartment. Took care of the lawn. Everything from washing windows to going to the grocery store. I stayed pretty busy. It was a legitimate job. I was paid a salary.

Q. Where are you getting food from now?

J. At OPCC on Colorado. They have morning feedings from 9:00 to 10:30. You get a bag lunch. There's an agency that at 4:00 o'clock they pass out burgers. They go to McDonald's and buy those dollar burgers and give you one.

Q. Where do you sleep?

J. I am sleeping here and there. I can't be more specific about that. Just where I can lay down, feel reasonably safe.

Q. What do you do about clothes?

J. All I have is the clothes on my back. I need clothes. That's one reason I came up here. I thought maybe I'd be able to go to a thrift store. At the Salvation Army, for a few bucks, you can get a clean pair of pants. I'm not earning any money these days. None.

Q. Do you panhandle?

J. No, I don't panhandle. I just can't do it. Too embarrassed. I don't bother anybody.

Q. What's a typical day for you?

J. A typical day for me—well, I do a lot of reading at the library. I pray. I do a lot of walking.

Q. Ever have any trouble with the Police?

J. No, no Police trouble. I just kind of stick to myself. I've had no problems. This is the first time I've been homeless. I think constantly about getting back to Florida. I've exhausted every possible avenue for getting money. I'm hoping that in Riverside I can get a ride back. I want to get a job, have a small room. If I could just get by and be independent…

Q. If you could, what would you have done differently?

J. If I had to do things differently, I would have applied myself more in my twenty's and kept a job and made a foundation for myself.

JANEEN

Janeen is a Caucasian woman with shoulder length blond hair, and a seasoned complexion. She dresses well. She is forty-one years old and is from Texas.

Q. When did you first become homeless, Janeen?

J: I was nineteen when I first became homeless. I was into drugs, and my mother knew. I was in and out of mental and substance abuse hospitals. This lasted for about three hundred and eighty days. Back at home again, they asked me to leave. I was going to see my grandmother and they had filed a lunacy petition on me. I hitchhiked on eighteen wheelers to Florida, then to California and to New York.

When I was in the hospital they put me in a halfway house in Texas, and I got a job. That was the last time I was in a home then. Then I met this guy and we split. His name was Robert. We went to North Dakota. There was a blizzard there; we had no money and no gas. Robert then asked me to do tricks for drugs. I said, "Fuck you, I'm not going to do tricks for you." And then he told me to split.

Q. What did you do then?

J. I came to California. One day I was in Anaheim at a big truck stop. I was walking down the street and I started crying. This truck driver came over and talked to me, and then he took me over to his cousin's house where I met this guy. After awhile I married him and had three kids by him. I had a lot of nice things. Nice jewelry, diamond rings, clothes and a car. I was working at a job. I didn't think that anything was good enough for me. I was like ripping my clothes up. We managed a small motel. I was there for about five years. We did a lot of drugs. Then I split and left the kids.

The longest I was homeless for was in the eighties and early nineties—four or five years. I was getting social security. My payee was giving me about two hundred a week. I just had a need to leave, you know.

At the holidays I go to the feedings for the homeless, and they always give you clothes. I still eat out of trash cans, you know. I don't go to recycle stuff, you know. Whenever I go out on long walks I look for stuff. Dumpster diving. People throw away mattresses and couches.

I had an apartment for about a year until just a little while ago. I left a candle going when I went out. The place caught fire and like my television melted. The clothes I could save were really smelly. I washed them at the laundry mat (sic). They made me move out so now its November 2002 and I'm homeless again period. I am waiting for February when Curley (social worker) will get me a section eight and I can get a new place.

Q. How are you going to pull yourself up this time?

J. I can sell women's clothes, and some friends of mine want me to go to cosmetology school because I do makeup very well, and maybe I can get a job using makeup. Sometimes when I think about it, maybe I could have been in modeling.

Q. Where do you sleep?

J. Now I sleep in business driveways. I have a blanket and I stash it. It's hard to find a hiding place for my stuff. People would turn me on to places. I was carrying around too much stuff and they helped me hide it. I usually have homeless friends that help me out. I would hide stuff in bushes and trash bins. I sleep in parking lots and driveways. Sometimes I sleep out by the dumpsters in alleys.

Q. How do you get by from day to day?

J. My money usually goes for food and stuff. I like Chinese food. I also like McDonald's. I spend some of my days in group therapy meetings. Sometimes I sleep with a guy for supper.

MICHAEL D.

Michael is a small Caucasian man with long salt and pepper hair and a long mustache. He is fifty-seven years old.

Q. Why did you become homeless, Michael?

M. I came down here about a year ago from Seattle. I'm a Psychotherapist by trade with about thirty-three years in the field. I got a call in Seattle about a year ago from a woman who said that she couldn't find my brother. I asked, "Who is this?" And she told me her name. She said,"I run the facility where your father is." I said, "What facility? My father lives in a condo in Santa Monica." She said, "No, he doesn't. He's with us." And she told me my brother had placed him in this extended care facility down in Huntington Beach and that he didn't have long to live, and that I should get down there quickly, so I did.

I gave my clients at the time to some trusted colleagues and left. I came down here and spent my father's last seventeen days on the planet with him. Over time I came to find that my twin brother was a deeply pathological individual and had sold literally everything that my father owned 'cause he had power of attorney, and was the executor of the estate, and over time had my father sign literally everything over to him.

They had manufactured a new Will thanks to an attorney who owed my brother money through gambling. My brother was a pathological gambler. He wrote me out of the Will. Not only did he steal everything from my father including all of his bank accounts, but all the money out of his insurance policies. Stole even the money from his funeral fund so that I ultimately paid for his funeral. So, there was nothing left.

Four days after my father's funeral my son in Colorado, he and his best friend were hit by a drunk driver. So much of the remainder of my funds had to go to Colorado to pay for my son's MRI and CAT scans, and what have you. This was about eleven months ago. I'm not going back to Seattle because I'm burnt out. I was just not admitting to myself that I was burnt out.

Q. What are your plans now?

M. Right now I'm in the process of helping a couple of friends put together a corporation that's going to be really huge when it hits. It's just taking some time to get off the ground.

I'm fortunate that I've got thirty five years of martial arts training behind me, and doubly fortunate in that I've been a therapist for thirty-three years. So both of those trainings combined helped me a great deal. It helped me adapt to this desperate poverty. The adaptation I needed to deal with this unbelievable rage, and the desolation of the loss of my father and my twin brother. My brother left with roughly 4.8 million dollars of my money. Hence the situation I'm in now.

Q. Are you getting any financial assistance?

M. I get GR now, which amounts to roughly $208 dollars a month and approximately $85 a month in food stamps or something like that. Once in awhile a friend of mine will buy me lunch. I had clothes when I came down here.

Q. Where do you sleep?

M. Lately I've been apartment sitting for a friend of mine. I did have a car. When I found out my brother wasn't going to be driving me around, I bought this piece of crap car for like six hundred bucks that I thought I would just have here in California and then go home to Seattle, before I was acknowledging the realities of the situation. Essentially I just stayed in the car. I slept in the car. It got impounded about two and a half weeks ago. So that was an ending.

Q. Have you tried to get work?

M. I've had forty seven job interviews, basically in my field or around it. But no one will hire me I find, for two reasons: my experience and my age. I am asked an illegal question roughly eighty percent of the time, which is "Michael, why is it a man your age is seeking a position like this?" Typically it's for a therapy position at an agency. And I say "Excuse me, you just asked me an illegal question. You can't ask a question based on my age." Typically it's a young person, and generally it's been a woman perhaps twenty-seven or eight years old. She is usually the director of the agency or the office manager or what have you. And she says, "You have no witnesses do you?" and she just smiles at me.

Q. What's a typical day for you?

M. I spend a good deal of time at the Coffee Bean up on Wilshire, and have met a great number of fine people. I've connected to some people with whom I am getting the business together that I told you about. I've also connected to some folks who, can we say, have needed some psychotherapeutic expertise. I have provided some of that in exchange for lunch or breakfast or dinner.

Q. Have you ever had to protect yourself out here?

M. Oh yes, seven times. Periodically I have been jumped by a couple of young men who thought I had money because I was carrying this cell phone. I've had to defend myself. I fought them. I hurt them. I studied two arts, Tai quando and Kung Fu.

Q. Ever had a problem with the police?

M. I had a little police trouble. When I had my car and was parking close to the Coffee Bean for many months. And I actually made friends with many of the police who came into the Coffee Bean. They were kind enough to tell me that they were getting complaints about where I was parking because people in that area would see me either sleeping in the car or getting up out of the car in the mornings. They found that peculiar enough to call it in. The police began to warn me and told me I needed to get past the Santa Monica border into West L.A.

Q. Have you had any medical problems?

M. Well, yes I have—October 7th of last year. Um, let me go back a few frames. At the end of September I had been getting my medication through a wonderful place called the Venice Family Clinic. I've been fighting a seizure disorder. They'd see me for free. They've provided medications but they ran out of medications. And for a short period of time they gave me what essentially is the medication I was on years ago that never worked.

I was frustrated and in tears, and I said, "This is not going to work, I'm going to have a seizure." And they said they're sorry and there's nothing they can do. And I said, "Mark my words. Eight to ten days from now I'm going to have a seizure." Nine days later on October 7th I was sitting in the delicatessen having a cup of coffee and I had a grand mal. They called the paramedics. The paramedics came and put me in the ambulance. As they were starting to drive away I had a heart attack. Fortunately the person in back knew what to do. My heart stopped and he put the electrodes on me.

They got me to UCLA. My heart stopped again. They put the electrodes on me again. When I got in they said they had to open me up in a hurry, so they did. They found one complete occluded artery, and put a balloon in and a stint, and so far so good. I got my seizure medication back, which is a wonderful medication called Topamax. It's a gift from God. It's the best! I've never had a seizure on it ever.

I still have concerns about my son in Colorado who is still recuperating from being hit by that driver. I stay in touch with him. I am probably going to lose my cell phone tomorrow or as we speak—right at 5:00 o'clock, unless a miracle happens. I can't make the $68 payment they want. That will be hard because we're both as close as a father and son can me. He's my hero. My son's a hero. He was the best thing that ever happened to me.

When this business that I told you about pops in the next two or three years, this will be between one and half and three billion dollars a year organization. That will enable all of us to do what we want to do for the people, not just what I can do with my son. But I'll be able to do with the homeless what I want to do, as well as AIDS victims. As a therapist I've got maybe four hundred names up on the AIDS quilt. Three hundred and seventy-seven clients and twenty-three friends that died from AIDS.

JACK P.

Jack is a twenty-four year old Caucasian man of medium height, with dark brown hair and a poor complexion.

Q. How did you first become homeless?

J. I was evicted from my apartment in May, 2001. I had the apartment for two and a half months, and I could not pay the rent so they asked me to leave. I was then in my car for two and a half months, and that got impounded. That was in June, 2001. My car was taken and I was forced to live on the street. I am now sleeping at the shelter. I'm trying to get employed by going to the Chrysalis Center. They find work for people like me.

Q. How was your childhood?

J. I was pretty much the runt of the litter when I was a little kid. Um, I kind of had a pretty difficult time growing up. When I was little in Nursery School and Kindergarten I was pretty much the runt of the litter. I actually got molested when I was six. And that has led to psycho trauma at this point in my life. But from that point on, up until I found Jesus Christ, those were the issues. Up until age six my life was pretty easy. After being molested things were pretty tough for me at that point. I was really having psychological issues.

Q. How did you do in school?

J. I did fairly well all throughout elementary. Junior High school I slacked off. I was sort of reclusive in my junior and senior years of High School.

Q. Where do you get food these days?

J. At the shelter where they provide breakfast and dinner. They serve a good dinner. I'm also pretty crafty. There are a lot of places downtown where I can get food. I'm also on GR, and I get food stamps right now. And I work as a food demonstrator. So I have some source of income. That's only on an on-call basis right now.

Q. As a food demonstrator, where do you work?

J. I work at a Supermarket. I set a table and offer food samples to people

Q. Do you live at the shelter now?

J. The shelter has been my residence the last two months. Before that I was in St. Vincent's shelter downtown. They serve a good breakfast, and they serve dinner. It's a very Catholic place there. They have a nice picture of St. Paul.

Q. Do you get your clothes at the shelter?

J. I've had some clothes provided to me from different places. Sometimes I get them from the shelter. I also got clothes at the Community Center. This pair of jeans I am wearing was given to me by a Priest.

Q. Do you panhandle at all?

J. I used to. It's not necessary at this point as I'm not in dire need for things. When I was sleeping on the street I would periodically take a bus to the shopping centers and I would panhandle. That was over a year ago though.

Q. What's a typical day for you?

J. I try to go to Church every day. These days I'm employment bound. I'm just trying to get a full time job so I can get back into society. I'm trying to be as responsible as I can.

Q. Have you ever had to protect yourself out on the street?

J. Yes, I've been in situations where I've had to yell at people. I haven't been in really bad situations where people pull weapons on me or stuff like that. I've actually been able to avoid that. I was really good about winning the association of other homeless people. Despite the fact that I was sleeping on the street I still went to Church. I was shaving every day in public restrooms.

Q. Have you had any trouble with Law enforcement?

J. I have had them tell me to sleep in other areas. I was told to leave the park. This happened between three and six times.

Q. Have you ever had to seek medical attention?

J. Oh yes, plenty of times. But my health is good. I don't smoke. I'm at a pretty good status there. I've been to the doctor for colds and things like that. In November of last year I was coming down with very severe pneumonia and a really nice person took me down to see the doctor. If nobody had helped me I probably would have had to call the paramedics or 911. The woman was very generous. I believe she either paid herself, or she informed my mother for reimbursement. My mother lives nearby.

Q. What are your biggest concerns these days?

J. That's a tough question. I'm usually very complacent. I feel that most of my problems and necessities are being taken care of. I really don't have any significant worries.

I try to go to Church every day. My dream is nothing more than to fulfill God's will and to follow the teachings of my Lord Jesus Christ as best I can. Also, to preach the gospel to as many as I can. That's really all I desire in life.

Q. Is there anything you would have done differently?

J. A lot of stuff I would have done differently. I would have done what I could to alleviate being homeless. But consequently, after becoming homeless, I have become more religious which I think is a blessing for me. Perhaps if I had not encountered such diversity from getting evicted and stuff, I wouldn't have gone to Church as much. So I'm blessed that God has let me go to Church this much.

Q. Would you say that being homeless is rough?

J. Yes, it's very difficult. And the thing is, um, you know, I'm not going to walk up to someone who I have nothing to do with, who's not a friend of mine and share my joy with. But if someone cares about me I will share what my life has been like with them. I get enough to eat. I have a place to sleep and I get a shower every day. All the bare necessities of life are being taken care of. There is nothing more I really desire. I am poor, but I get the bare necessities.

DON H.

Don is a big, heavy black man. He is missing a few upper front teeth. He is very likable, very congenial. He is forty-five years old.

Q. Where are you originally from, Don?
D. San Antonio, Texas. I was born there but I was raised here in Los Angeles.
Q. Did you go to school in LA?
D. Yes I did.
Q. Did you get a High School diploma?
D. No, I didn't, Sir.
Q. When did you first become homeless?
D. Me and my wife were staying in Westchester. I became homeless when I was on alcohol and drugs. My wife left me. At first everything was going okay. I was working at Universal Studios as an usher. I worked in the Cineplex, where people are invited to review a movie. I lost that job because my wife would keep calling me, bugging me, so the manager had to let me go. I had another job working at "The Wave" newspaper. I was working there for about seventeen years. I would drop it off at houses, you know, throw it off the truck and stuff.
Q. What happened with the Wave job?
D. They laid us off.
Q. Tell me what your childhood was like, Don.
D. Well, when I was a little kid I used to have seizures and stuff. Yeah, I fell down the stairs, and my memory ain't too good you know. Also I'm slow at reading and writing. I had an okay childhood.
Q. How did you feel when you first became homeless?
D. Ah—hurt! I was very hurt, yeah. I didn't know what to do. Ah, you know, I couldn't find a job because of the prediction (sic) I was in. You know my reading and writing and stuff like that. I could hardly fill out the application and stuff. Yeah, and like I said, my memory ain't too good, you know, yeah.
Q. When you first became homeless where did your food come from?
D. The Midnight Mission downtown. I was homeless in Hollywood but I went downtown to eat.
Q. Where did you sleep?
D. I'd just ride a bus back and forth at night time. I'd sleep on the bus.
Q. What did you do for clothing?
D. Well, they had clothes at the drop in center. Out in LA I used to volunteer at this drop in center. I used to go there and wash the clothes, shower and stuff you know.

Q. Do you get any public assistance?

D. I'm on SSI now. I have been getting SSI most all along.

Q. I know that you are a prolific panhandler. How long have you been panhandling?

D. (laughs) Oh, man, a good eleven years—since I've been out here in Santa Monica.

Q. So what do you do to pass the time?

D. Well, sometimes my brother lets me come over to his house and stay. I don't like being by myself. Sometimes I go over there. Sometimes I just ride the bus all night.

Q. Have you had any altercations while on the street?

D. I remember when a guy got on the bus, he opens the windows and it's cold and I told him, I said, "Man, why don't you go on and close the windows."? So after that one thing led to another and we got into a fight. He really broke me up real bad cause I was drunk, you know. He beat me up real bad. He beat me up so bad I had to call the paramedics. They took me to the hospital and stuff you know. And ran test and stuff on me, but no bones were broken so they said I was very lucky.

Q. Did you call the Police?

D. Yeah, but they couldn't find him.

Q. Have you ever had trouble with the Police?

D. Oh, what, since I've been here in Santa Monica? Well, yes, like tickets and stuff. Like no smoking in the park and stuff like that, littering.

Q. Have you needed medical assistance here?

D. No, I go to a doctor in LA. I have insurance—the United Way. One time they said I had some kind of disease and stuff. After that I was treated and the stuff, it just kind of went away. And the seizures, sometimes I still have them.

Q. Are they like epilepsy?

D. Yes, uh huh, you know this foam to the mouth you know.

Q. What is your biggest concern now?

D. I worry about my kids, and I worry about myself being out here for this long, eleven years you know.

Q. What are the ages of your children?

D. The oldest one is about fifteen. And I got another one thirteen and the boy is about nine. Two girls and a boy. They live in Las Vegas.

Q. Do you give them any support?

D. Yes, I do. I give them about $500 a month out of my SSI.

Q. What would you like to be doing?

D. I would sure like to live in a family's house. Have a good job like have. You know, cause I haven't been homeless my whole life. I used to have nice things and stuff. Nice car, nice house and a wonderful job. But things have happened because of the predicament I'm in.

Q. You want to go back to work again?

D. Of course, oh yeah.

Q. Do you have any girl friends?

D. Well yes. I had one in Pasadena. I don't know what happened to her cause we broke up in 1986. I didn't give her nothing for Valentine's Day so she thought I didn't care about her. I have had some little female friends where I used to go over to their house and stuff. One thing led to another, but we weren't really going together you know.

Q. What's the hardest part of living on the street?

D. Well, it seem like when you're living on the streets, people, you know, they look at you like you're nobody. Like your life is just scrap. And there ain't no hope. But there is hope you know. The hope is that someday I can find a job and get off the streets. I need people to help me out with the application. I need people to help me read and write the stuff like that you know. I'll be alright you know. One thing will lead to another.

HELENA T.

Helena is a black woman of medium height. She has braided hair under a yellow scarf. She is forty-nine years old.

Q. When did you become homeless?

H. I first became homeless in March of this year, approximately four months ago.

Q. Why are you homeless?

H. I just got out of touch with reality. Those people in the hotel I stayed at for two years. They were playing mind control trips on me. You know what I mean? Now, I don't know if I want to go to a hotel apartment again. You know, where there's other people that are strange. The hotel was like for drug addicts and prostitutes. It was called The Olympic Hotel. I paid my rent all the time like clockwork. There were a lot of people I had to call the Police on all the time, and I just couldn't take it all the time.

I got scared and I left to live on the street. I was in the hospital first for two months and when I got out I stayed in one of those flimsy hotel places in Hollywood with those crack heads. Now, I live outside of a bank called Washington Mutual. I've been there for three months. There are a lot of us who live there. It's awesome. They let us stay in front of the bank. Then we get up at 6:00 A.M. and go.

Q. Tell me something about your past.

H. The last thirty years of my life has been ethereal, heavy duty. I'm a Scientologist really. I was a Scientologist thirty years ago, and then I became a Christian. Yeah, I was in it. The people were really nice to me. They are still nice. Scientologists are nice people. They're awesome. I wrote a hundred page book that I call the Holy Grail. It's about life and stuff. I think I'm a chosen one, for love.

Q. What about your childhood?

H. My childhood wasn't bad. Emotionally, yes. My dad was an alcoholic and my mom was gay. My dad kicked my mom out. My dad was an alcoholic. He was in the Marine Corps. He died of cancer. I still see my mom once in awhile. When I was twenty, my mother took me to Patton and I was diagnosed as manic depressive and bipolar. Back and forth, back and forth.

Q. How did you do in school?

H. Excellent. I was on the Honor Roll. I was raised in Orange county. I excelled in school, man. In sports I always had A's. I was like a B average in school. I went to Junior College and took dance, voice, and music theory. I took up acting. I flunked music theory 'cause I didn't like it.

Q. How did you feel when you first became homeless?

H. It jarred my mind. Now I'm used to it. I have Social Security you know. I've had that all my life. I just don't feel like getting into a place. As for food outlets, I have a list of these.

Q. What about clothes?

H. All I have is the clothes I have on—some jeans and a sweatshirt.

Q. Do you ever panhandle?

H. No, I won't panhandle. I have a lot of pride. I'm real moralistic. I don't take drugs and I don't smoke. I'll take a drink once in awhile. No addictions. I'm not promiscuous.

Q. What's a typical day for you?

H. I walk seven miles in the morning. It takes me about one and a half hours. Then I go to the library. Then I see people at the food line I know.

Q. Have you ever had to protect yourself?

H. I've been hit by three guys. They kicked me. I called the cops, too. It's because I stick up for myself. I guess my voice is powerful. I don't hit. I'm not into violence. This girl betrayed me so I verbally said things to her. This guy went to stand up for her. I said things to him too. He just came up and kicked me. And then I called the cops. They came and got him.

Q. Any trouble with the Police yourself?

H. Oh no, they like me. Like I don't cause trouble. I'm gonna be fifty, Dude. I just got back from my Psychiatrist. This year, January and February, I was in the nut house at Kaiser in Chinatown.

Q. Do you have any dreams for the future?

H. Huh, my dreams? Getting married, having two kids even though I've had a hysterectomy. Get married to a movie star, actor, 'cause that's what I was doing thirty years ago. It's gonna happen and that's not just my sickness talking, you know.

Q. What would you have done differently?

H. I would want a different mom and dad. I'm getting tired. I should get a place. I'm too old to be doing this.

ROBERT Y.

Robert is an Englishman. He's a large man with white hair and beard in need of a cut. He is wearing dirty clothes and smells. He is fifty-four years old, and admits to being manic-depressive. Robert is full of windy tales.

Q. Robert, where are you originally from?

R. I originally originate from El Paso, Texas. And I came out here to Los Angeles.

Q. Where did you get your English accent?

R. My English accent was due to being a naturalized citizen. I came over here in the 50's with a guardian. My parents were in the Air Force, and my mother was an English teacher. They were killed in England in an automobile accident. So I was turned over to a guardian. Then I went to Atlanta, Georgia, and I had to do a little while in Juvenile hall while they figured out guardianship on me. They were data processing my guardianship as an American citizen. I had to take the oath of allegiance in South Hampton. And to reinstate a U.S. passport to come over here because of the Air Force personnel.

Q. What were you doing in Texas?

R. This time I came from Texas. I was the graveyard shift manager at the El Paso rescue mission. And, uh, I called up a friend here in California and I asked him to check on a driver's license situation. And the strange thing about it was that he said that I had data processed an automobile accident in the State of California. And technically the Santa Monica police believed I was dead.

And so I terminated myself at the graveyard shift manager position. I went to Las Cruses, New Mexico. And uh, I got off the Greyhound bus and I went over to the Gospel mission where I had some business. When I got off the Greyhound bus I was sitting at McDonald's and having breakfast. A minister walked up to me, and his name was—

Q. Bob, just a moment. Let's get back to business. How long ago did you become homeless?

R. I became homeless in let's see, 2001. I replaced myself as a member of the El Paso rescue mission. I was on salary there.

Q. What kind of education have you had?

R. I had private school in England, and then I went to public school in Wilmington, North Carolina.

Q. When you first became homeless, how did you feel?

R. It was a rather hard decision. I was limited on income. I didn't have a lot of money. I data processed a group of people who were homeless themselves through circumstances and I ran into them at the Gospel Mission. And, uh, based on their advice, I changed my lifestyle. I decided to do the Mission program for awhile. I became oriented to Theology and Sociology because they had access to society irregardless of the fact that they were homeless citizens. In other words, society ordained their lifestyle as being acceptable. Within the framework of walking around in the public, because of the theory of teenagers. Teenage females and teenagers in particular, because of the rape crisis situation. So to be a homeless citizen one has to be trustworthy around available female contacts you know. So they have a set standard policy of sociological values, set aside by society as being acceptable.

Q. Where are you sleeping these days?

R. I'm staying in a spot where a friend of mine had. He's in jail right now. His name is Fred, and I'm watching his spot for him. It's near the Medical Center.

Q. Where are you getting clothing these days?

R. I go to the Drop in Center. And I go to a place called the Pink Onion.

Q. Are you receiving SSI at this time?

R. I have filed for a UA 1 disability with the State of California, which is considered SSD, Social Security Disability. And based on an accident report, I went to a hospital here and found a medical portfolio that's under the authority of Dr. Wise, and uh, then with that I went to the State disability people on Wilshire Blvd. and they sent me downtown.

I received a portion of the payment just before Christmas. I got one hundred and twenty dollars from Mr. Williams at the department there. But he said I won't get a formal check until they complete the medical reports and everything. They told me the exact amount and said maybe sixty days. I was injured in this car accident business on the promenade when that guy mowed through the Farmer's market and killed 10 people and injured a bunch more. I'm victim number thirty-eight. That's what they had me listed as.

Q. So how do you spend you time?

R. Basically I get up in the morning, I get washed up. I go to the doughnut shop, get a cup of coffee, a doughnut. I get washed up in the restroom. I check my laundry—see if it has to be done. Then basically I make telephone calls if I have to make them. Then I walk on down to the promenade down here for exercise. I take medication. I panhandle for food and everything. Get a couple of bucks and just keep myself busy.

I have some friends. Once in a while I'll go down to the beach and crush cans and bottles go up to the Union 76. I just keep myself busy while I'm putting things together. I eat at McDonald's. I go to Savon, and I use the hot water facilities and the clothing facilities at OPCC. I also found out that the Sheriff department has my I.D., and they also have an automobile on me. A deputy sheriff by the name of C.Y. Smith has I.D. on me. So I'm negotiating right now with the Sheriff department until I get my I.D. released.

Q. Have you seen a doctor since the accident at Farmer's Market?

R. Yeah, I went to a doctor here as a matter fact, UCLA. Well the police had me listed a DOA and the Fire department did not argue over my life. This is after the accident, but the strange thing about it was when I was in El Paso, as I explained to you, I was not aware of the fact that I had been in an accident in the State of California so, in theory of the orbit of a comet, when I left El Paso I came out here.

All of a sudden I was in a wheelchair. And that was a fact. But when I crossed the State line of California I was an extremely ill person. And so I had to go to the hospital here. And, uh, I was picked up. I went to the Rescue Mission in Blythe and they called Ampuserve on me, and I went to the hospital in Blythe. They put me in cerebral palsy status, ah, division. I don't have cerebral palsy but those were the symptoms.

Q. What is your biggest concern today?

R. My biggest worry is law enforcement actually because I don't want to render myself into becoming a criminal nature, or becoming a criminal within that framework. Because in this state of being they could designate someone being an unlawful person, based on their daily social habits. And because of the jurisprudence of it, I have to maintain myself outside of their determination of a prisoner.

So I had to do away with the criminal nature of myself. So that's my main concern, staying out of being a criminal. But if I don't get it settled, I can't get my I.D. back from the Sheriff because of an investigation going on. I don't think I'm going to remain in the State of California any more than maybe the summer of this year.

Q. Do you have anything to look forward to?

R. You mean when I go back home? I'm going back to El Paso actually. Basically I'll be working out of El Paso. I do a number of things. I have some friends in Arizona and we do construction work, this and that. I've been working on—ah—I have an engineering degree as a matter of fact from the State of California, San Francisco. And I've worked for labs—Nuclear labs, as a research individual. Sub atomic particles.

And so my education is from the state of California. I came out here and went to the University. And, went to Hills College of engineering, and various other engineering companies. I left California in the late seventies when there was a decline in the need of engineers. And I moved out to Texas. I moved to Houston as a matter of fact.

And so I left Houston and moved to El Paso because of the engineering market out there. And that was the reason for joining the Rescue Mission out there. But, I've had problems. See I'm a naturalized individual and to be listed I have to maintain my immigration status with the US Government. And I can't be listed as DOA somewhere.

ARCHI

Archi is a forty year old black male about 5'11", with a beard that is mostly grey.

Q. Archi, where are you from?

A. From Los Angeles. I grew up in Hollywood.

Q. What education have you had?

A. I went to four different schools in Hollywood. I graduated from Hollywood High School.

Q. How did you become homeless?

A. I was living with some friends about five years ago, and it was really convenient for the amount of money that I got from Social Security. It was a two bedroom place. A couple of the people had to move. They went on to different things, so we couldn't keep the place by ourselves so that was that. After that I started going from motel to motel, but motels are too expensive so I ended up homeless.

Q. Do you have a job resume?

A. Primarily restaurant work. Like cooking and waiting tables. I've managed a dining hall and a delicatessen. That was in '83 and '84.

Q. What keeps you from doing the same thing today?

A. I'm bi-polar and manic depressive. I have episodes.

Q. Have you done any jail time?

A. Yeah.

Q. Does that make it harder to find employment?

A. Yeah, I imagine it would, but I haven't worked in a long time. Just odd jobs. I've been in jail because of mostly warrants.

Q. What kind of tickets did you get?

A. Jay walking tickets that I didn't take care of, and sleeping in doorways and stuff like that. The biggest thing was for sales. I was selling rock cocaine. That was the biggest jail time, but the other stuff was just tickets. A cigarette butt ticket for putting my cigarette out on the promenade. That was my last ticket, and that turned into a warrant. I did some time for that one. I did twenty-two months for the rock.

Q. Did you have a good childhood?

A. Yeah, I really can't complain so much. My parents were divorced when I was really young. I lived with my aunt for a little while when I was about four. And, ah, then my mom came and got me and I lived with her. She suffered from schizophrenia. She had an episode, and from that my dad got custody of me. I primarily grew up with my father, and I would see my mother on weekends. I had two different families. I had a step-mother and a step-father. All in all I really can't complain.

Q. Do you still get along with your father?

A. Yeah, yeah. We don't talk that much but we get along good.

Q. Where do you get your meals these days?

A. There are a few different facilities in the area. Um, Salvation Army, OPCC, feedings in the park, and there's a really nice meal on Monday and Tuesdays in Beverly Hills.

Q. How about your clothes?

A. About the same places I get my meals. The Salvation Army gives me a voucher which I use to get my clothes at their store. They have a drop-in center where you can get lunch, bus tokens, and other things.

Q. Where are you sleeping?

A. Wherever I can find a spot. (Laughs) It's been kinda rough because in the last two years a lot of places that were okay to sleep, and of course when it rains you especially want a place with an overhang, they've started to post signs that you can't sit or sleep there. If you do it's legal for the Police to give you a ticket or arrest you.

Q. How long have you been receiving SSI?

A. Since about 1986.

Q. Have you earned any money lately, or have you panhandled?

A. No and no.

Q. Have you ever had to protect yourself?

A. Surprisingly no. I have had my bags taken. I set them down and when I woke up they were gone. (Laughs)

Q. What do you do with yourself during the day?

A. That's pretty easy. I wake up, go to the park, go get a shower, come back to the park. Pretty much stay at the park, and then, go to sleep.

Q. Have you had any medical emergencies?

A. Um, I sprained my ankle really bad one time out here. I mean really bad. What happened was I was running and there was this wall about three feet high. I'm thinking that the other side is the same depth. So I hopped the wall, and the other side was like eight feet down. (Laughs) That was the stupidest thing I ever done in my life. My ankle was about the size of a grapefruit. The paramedics took me to the hospital. My Medi-Cal took care of it.

Q. What concerns do you have?

A. I'm kind of concerned about, I've been really trying to go after Section Eight housing, and just found out it's defunct now. There is no more Section Eight. That's really bugging me.

(Author's note: There is a freeze on Section Eight for six months as of this writing.)

Q. Do you have any hopes?

A. Yeah, I think like, you know, to get into the position of—well, I'd like to go back to school. I would like to get into the position of having a full time job.

Q. What kind of job?

A. A paralegal.

Q. Is there anything you would have done differently with your life?

A. No.

Q. What is your view of the world right now?

A. Disassociation. People seem to be more disassociated from people. I don't want to say things are colder. That's just what I see.

Q. What keeps you going?

A. Hope. Hope that the next day is better than today. Keeping sight of my dreams. Being optimistic.

MICHAEL W.D.

Michael is a forty-nine year old black man, about 5'11", with some weight on him. He has a shaved head.

Q. Michael, is it okay to use your name?

M. Well, Michael D., I guess. You know what—why don't you use my whole name, Michael Wayne Dancy. Your book's gonna sell. So I want to be part of that. Don't ask me how I know, I just know.

Q. Thank you Michael. I have a question. Is there any particular reason why you have your head shaved?

M. It's easier when you're living outside to have a shaved head so that way bugs and stuff don't get on you. You know, lice can't get under your skin. I don't have to wake up in the morning to scratch. I just keep it clean.

Q. Where are you from originally?

M. Springfield, Massachusetts. I came here in April, 1974. I was living in Pasadena where I became a college student, and I wanted to go into the Navy. I was a pre-med student. But I didn't realize I had an alcohol problem. I started that at age thirteen.

My mother used to have a lot of parties, and big gallons of liquor in the house. I used to sneak and steal it. Then on Friday and Saturday nights from school I would go to house parties and we'd get drunk to go party. And, it became a thing that everything I do I had to get loaded. So I brought that with me. And, it started out okay, but it just seems like every time I would use I'd get in trouble. Eventually a friend of mine told me that I needed to get some help but I didn't listen.

This was about '74 or '75. I came out here in '74. An old lady, she told me, I need to get some help. This was on the campus. She came back one day and told me I had to take a business administration class just to have in case the other thing didn't do well.

My friends told me they had friends who skated through Med school with speed and Cannibis and other things because of the pressure of med school. Well, one thing led to another and I realized that I couldn't handle pressure. I found out that to go to med school I had to study 500 to 700 pages of study materials a night to be ready for class in the morning. It was enormous. But, I love medicine and I love hospital work, and I love helping people and serving. I love all those things that come with it. But I wasn't ready for the pressure that med school brings.

So, I went to an AA thing. I tried that out for awhile. It didn't work because I didn't want to hear someone else tell me that I was screwing up, that I was sick, that I was incapable of running my own life. I thought I was doing well. So, I ended up going to County General Hospital. Because of the pre-med thing, they gave me a job as a nurses' attendant. That's bedpan work. I moved up in different ranks and stuff in the hospital. The hospital liked me and I liked them.

I had a girlfriend that was a doctor from Bangladesh. This was in '79 or '80. She was cool and I liked her, and I had some friends that graduated from other countries doing internship at UC Medical Center, and they helped motivate me more. And then they had a minorities program; med core program, and if you kept your grades up they would take care of your expenses, because at that time it was $20,000 a semester. Where is a poor child like me gonna get $20,000? 80ooo

So, I moved up, got into that and then eventually I failed again. I ended up downtown in skid row. This is now '81 or '82. Crack cocaine started coming out then. I ended up laying around there and became addicted. All these times I had been in and out of jail.

Q. What were you in jail for?

M. Either for panhandling or for stealing something. I didn't mention that in my early life I was in reform school. I used to steal cars before I came to California—when I was a little kid, fourteen, fifteen, sixteen years old. Stealing cars, that was a hot thing for kids then. GTOs. I would just drive them. It wasn't to make money. It was just for the speed of them. How fast you could go, how you would get away from the police. American Legion Highway was a dragster place. And it was a cool thing for whoever could use a screwdriver and pop the ignition, to get into a car in thirty seconds and could get away. And so I went to Lyman School for boys. Then I went to a Catholic school. I was not quite seventeen years old. Right about that time is when I moved to California from Massachusetts.

In 1986 I was in downtown Los Angeles, in jail, coming out of jail again. I went to a mental health place because I was trying to get SSI. Just kept on hanging out on the street and in the park, and that's where I slept. I stayed with all of us smoking crack. The crack dealer was nearby. I did that for two or three years till they cracked down on the crack cocaine business. If you're caught dealing or doing this you could get life for dealing. They were just getting serious about it. I was out of hand.

Q. What did you do about it?

M. I was in downtown Los Angeles. I was staying in this hotel. And the coke dealers told me that I got to pay protection, and I got to buy drugs while I was staying at the hotel and have sex with their fifteen and sixteen year old whores.

The old men loved 'em. They'd get their railroad pension checks, military pension checks, pension checks from their jobs. And this is money that they really don't need, so they'd buy whores, buy drugs, just to pass the time.

For me they told me that I had to pay for protection just like everybody else or get thrown out a window, or somebody's gonna kick my door in. This happened in January of this year, 2004. So I told them I can't pay this 'cause I don't have the money so I'm going to leave. They said, "Okay, but you better be gone! You'd better make sure because you better get gone." I landed in Santa Monica on the 27th.

I ran into a whole bunch of people who wanted to tell me about this program or that program. I went into the shelter in February, and the director told me with her body guard that I had to leave. They didn't tell me why. So, here I am now. I'm on the street, and I'm just like really angry and upset but I'm doing fine. But I'm upset and I'm fed up with shelters and this whole line about helping you out. I'm just going to save my money. When you got enough money saved you can be clean. I can wash up out there on the pier, you know, I can lay down here and get a better living arrangement, something more cushiony, and I'm gonna change this around. Still trying to be a high class homeless person. I'm forty-nine years old, where am I gonna go?

Q. How are you surviving now?

M. I eat at the different food outlets, Salvation Army, a Church, and then people feed us in the park. So you know I have plenty of food going on there. I can save my little GR check, I don't have to spend it. Cause I want to get a mobile home but that's far off. But I'm still gonna save.

Q. How do you clean your clothes?

M. I wash my clothes when I take a shower and I let them dry on me. Then I have some deodorant that they give me at one of the centers.

Q. Have you been panhandling?

M. I don't want to do that 'cause you can go to jail. Everything you do is a ticket.

Q. Do you worry about other people?

M. Yes, they are always going into my stuff, stealing my stuff. And now that I've told the police about it, I'm a snitch. I have to be careful now. I can't sleep too much in the night. I can't sleep too much in the day. I have find places where I'm safe.

Q. What would you like to do now?

M. I'd like to go to culinary school. I can cook a little bit but I want to improve that. I don't want to do it for a job. But I want to do it someday when I get a home and I can really burn, really cook. I'm talking about shaving macadamia nuts and make a butter and put that on your chicken and then fry the chicken—knowing how to de-bone a chicken, put it in a food processor and mix it with eggs and bell peppers and onions and make a great omelet. I'd also like a garden. I like to grow things. But I can't do that. You know I'm scared to do that out here. I have to get me a place. Maybe get myself a mobile home in Malibu if I ever get that close to you. I'm not going to steal it, you know.

Q. Have you had any girlfriends?

M. I don't want no sex! Sex right now, that is a bad thing. For one thing, women are not responsible. Most of them that are out there and most of them that are not out there don't want anything to do with me because I'm homeless. You know, it would be nice to just slow down and have a nice girlfriend you could just lay on the ground with, but where has she been? She's gotta have money, she's gotta have things. People proposition her—especially the ones that look like they're working. They give it up so they can have drugs and money—have the little things that they wanted. They see a nice dress in the shop that they want. They're homeless, they say "damn, I think I deserve that." So they're gonna open their ass for somebody. Sex is definitely the bottom of the totem pole.

Q. Do you have any friends?

M. Friends in the street, no. Because everybody has a different agenda. They're criminals. They can't be trusted. They don't give a damn about you. So there's nothing going on as far as true trust, friendship and understanding. It's with the Minister where you get food. That's my connection for friendship.

Q. How does the world look to you these days?

M. There's something going on. It's very secret, but it's going on. They're changing the plant life; they're changing the animal life. There are a whole lot of other things going on that they can't tell us about because it would cause a panic.

This world is not going to be destroyed by a nuclear holocaust. This world is going to be destroyed with viruses. Dangerous, deadly, serious viruses—that are so intelligent that man cannot defeat them.

There's a lot of stuff coming into the country that cannot be controlled. There's a lot abroad that they're trying to control, keeping it from coming into this country. And AIDS is still destroying. There's other stuff that destroys, but they're not known like AIDS.

Q. Is there any place you'd feel safe?

M. I don't know, Robert. It's hard to say. The safest places I've found to go are Indian Reservations. They're all over the place. I came from Massachusetts, the Mohawk trail. I haven't been to any in California. I would go to Washington State and Oregon and up that way to Montana. Oklahoma's good, Mexico's good.

Q. Do you have any advice that you would give a person who has just become homeless?

M. I've told a couple of people, especially the women, that it's best to get into the day care center.

Lie, and tell them that you've been beat up by your husband or your boy friend, and that you're scared to go home, or that you have gangs that are looking for you. And that way you'll get immediate help. You can tell them that you've been under so much stress that you're nervous, and your mind is going, that you've had a nervous breakdown, you're scared everywhere you go, and that you have no health issues. You can get right in, and eat the good living food and get clothing and showers. Maybe they will help you get your SSI.

Q. What would you tell the guys?

M. It depends who you're talking to. Some of them are murderers. A lot of them are on the run. You don't want to talk to them. They'll kill you. They wait days, weeks, months, until they catch you going to sleep, and they'll cut your throat. Then there's those who are open for advice. I'd tell them where to wash, where they can sleep. The ocean is the best place to sleep because the police substation is there. Coastguard and K-9 patrol. You have to find yourself a hidden area on the beach. You have to find places where people can't find you. There are areas that are real dark. Sometimes the Coastguard will fly over you and shine the light on you, and they'll see you and then take the light off you and then disappear in the helicopter. It would be better than to sleep out here on the ground.

STEPHANIE V.

Stephanie is an adorable, Hispanic girl with cute brown hair, cut short. She is twenty-eight years old and lives in her truck.

Q. Why are you homeless, Stephanie?

S. I would have a nice—I would take care of myself. I'd work in the entertainment industry and shit like that. I worked for a good job that I can't like keep. These freaking jobs with their corporate bullshit with the little stuff I go through like Warner Brothers consumer products. It was weird. I saw the lady I worked with before when I worked for Para Communications. They do shipping and she was one of the studio stores who was a client and I worked for her, and I got contacts, you know, I got networked. I tried to get into that kind of work in entertainment 'cause I live in Burbank. And I'm working for the studio and it's awesome. She got me in and I seen her out on the beach today. It was a trip. I worked for DreamWorks Records in Beverly Hills.

I had a car, a nice truck. I had to like let go of that because of the payments. It started like going down hill, and I didn't care. It was a '99 Toyota Tacoma. I have this other car now—a jeep Cherokee. But at least I have transportation and I'm not walking and I'm doing my thing. I sometimes live with my family, my sister and brother-in-law. They're totally awesome and they help me. I was doing good. I was working but I didn't have my own space you know. I was like sharing the room with two kids. Well, hey, I can't complain right? They gave me something nobody would have given me. Like a chance like that. They gave me a lot and it was a nice area. It was like, they gave me help. I left because stuff wasn't going right.

I first became homeless because things weren't working out at home. Ever since I got my job at DreamWorks Records I was not communicating with my brother-in-law. They wanted me to be home at 10:00 o'clock every night. I'm twenty-eight years old. I've been through a lot of shit in my life. I been through things that you wouldn't even imagine. I choose to be out there 'cause I can't go home to my mom and dad. My brother's there. He's like not right. We've always been like rivals. It got very violent. It's an ongoing thing.

Q. Exactly how long have you been homeless?

S. I've been homeless since May, 2003. It sucks 'cause I've been in my fucking car. I was so depressed. I smoke pot and shit. I'm with this guy who is like homeless I guess, and he's driving me up the wall. I feel like I can succeed and have a job and friends right? I have to be clean now. I'm walking around all these beautiful people now and I mean this just isn't me. I have to get my shit straight. My birthday's gonna be sometime soon you know.

I'd like to do something for myself. I can't go back to my sister and brother-in-law. This was when I lost my job at DreamWorks. I was going to get my own apartment in Burbank, and then this lady that I knew from Savon over the years from buying stuff, she's like, ah, I'm an apartment manager. She said she had a single. Somebody else got that. I don't care. I was gonna get a small one just my own.

I don't want to live in this piece of shit truck. It's kind of crazy but, hey, I'm doing this and I'm feeling okay. Like a human being. All I want to do is go to the job and do a job like that. It's like, thanks a lot Dreamworks. I was doing such tedious stuff like, are you stamping the paper on the back of the page and not on the front of the receipt. Just little stupid shit. I collected unemployment for a long time. You're like my psychologist right now.

Q. How does it feel to be living on the street?

S. I felt real dirty when I was first out on the street. Dirty, ugly and stupid. Not right. I was a lazy bum. A good title for a book—The Lazy Bum.

Q. Where do you get food?

S. Well, like today, I had doughnuts and soda. This friend of mine gets food from his mother who lives in Sun Valley. Burbank has this agency. They give out food and lunches. They will give you a whole shopping cart if you need it. That's if you have a place to stay. They have tuna and shit like that. Some people have it worse than me. Being homeless, this isn't like me. I mean I just can't live at my house. Guys and the weird, you know the package, right? What do they want with a girl? They're like, "comeback tonight." Some dork will say, "Hey, you can take a shower here", or "Can I use your phone number for my resume?"

I've been trying to get a job. I always have these bullshit problems. I swear I don't know what I'm going to do. I try to stay clean and get my resume out there. I need a schedule. I don't have a life right now. I need to change the oil in my car. I need to be stronger. My mom tells me no one else will do something for you. You have to do it yourself. My biggest worry is that I'll turn thirty and not have a job.

Q. What dreams do you have for yourself?

S. I don't have any dreams. I need to grow up.

BRUCE M.

Bruce is a forty-four year old white male, about 5'10" tall. His hair is graying and needs a cut.

Q. Bruce, tell me about your childhood.

B. Oh yeah, I had great parents. My mother is still alive but she's in care right now. She's seventy-nine. I had a radical childhood. I'm an only child so I was given a lot of things. I grew up in a good area. I got involved with drugs in high school, and I went to college where it seemed to take control of my life. I was in a partying situation and my drinking got bad.

Q. Are you doing any 12-step programs now?

B. Yep. I'm trying to keep myself involved in the programs. I have a sponsor. You know I'm homeless. I'm still in the streets. When you say a cardboard box, well that's basically how I live. Whoever said homeless people don't work really hard—everything we do as homeless is work. I mean things like waking up and cleaning up wherever you slept the night before, or going to find things to eat. Not having transportation, not having money. It has definitely opened up my eyes to what it's like to get in touch with God.

I was born on Easter morning so I've always felt that God was in my life. I'm just not letting Him be in charge of what I do. The judgment calls for me you know. Getting in trouble is my inability to listen to God's word. I always think that I have the answer. My answer is that God has the plan. I don't have the plan. And that's what leads me to be on the streets, losing friends. My alcoholism is getting better. Whenever I drink incessantly everything caves in. I've been sporadically homeless.

Q. How long have you been homeless this time?

B. Three months. I used to call friends for help and a place to stay. They help me out for awhile, but they get tired of my drinking. You know when I drink it doesn't matter how close people are to me, I'll take advantage of them. Not steal, but I do things I normally wouldn't do. I don't know if that's what's contributing to the homelessness that I have. I mean I notice that lately I've had to push myself to go back to meetings no matter where they are. I always have some kind of excuse. I need to get myself to a point where I listen to God, and what God tells me to do, I do. No matter what, whatever I think. I want to do that. That's where my problem lies. It's rough being out there.

Q. Have you always lived in this area?

B. Yes.

Q. Where do you sleep?

B. In back behind the post office. I know a couple people that stay back there.

Q. Do you panhandle?

B. Well, I've been known to. I don't like doing it. Sometimes my depression will set in and I don't even want to ask someone.

Q. What do you do to pass the time?

B. Because I've always been an athlete, and I like to be a good shape, I like to do a little bit of workouts. I'll get in some programs or I'll take a nice shower down there at Swashlock.

Q. Have you had any trouble with the Police?

B. I've had trouble with the Police for DUI's. This has been in the last few years. I've had three DUI's. That's why I'm so concentrating now on totally restructuring my life; letting myself go to God. I can't afford to have any more problems in that area. I don't want to go to prison. Trying to let God run my life.

Q. How does the world look to you today?

B. It can be cold lately. The world's got a lot of problems. I get really frustrated reading the paper. The U.S. is going out and taking care of the rest of the world, and I'm looking at our own nation. We need to concentrate on what we're doing back on the home front. I'm happy that we have so much love and care for the rest of the world that we'd go out on a limb, but then I hear about these countries giving us a bunch of duff.

That's just on the political front. The world is what we make it I think. I have a pretty good outlook I think, even though I'm going through what I'm going through now. Some days when I wake up I have a positive attitude. Some days are more stagnant than others. I get depressed from time to time.

Q. Do you have anything to look forward to in your future?

B. I'd like to maybe do some things along the lines of what you've done. Maybe try to compile a set of stories from times when my life was less than grand. Maybe it would make it better for other people in the future who are suffering from these things. If they could read about someone who's been there, done that, maybe it would help them overcome the little bumps in the road.

Q. What advice would you give these people?

B. I'd say definitely get in touch with your higher power, and believe that He's your destiny in your life. When we think that we've got the answers, that's not listening to our higher power. He gets you over this great big rocky road that you go through. Stay in touch with programs that can offer benefits, advice and counseling; group therapy, and all kinds of medical services. Stay in touch with these organizations in the area or wherever you are, to overcome these hardships.

Homelessness can be lonely. There's an element of trouble there. In my opinion it's a place where you are that you can climb out of if you have a positive outlook. That you can seek these things that can help you get better again. Things that get you focused and pointed on a positive road that's going to take you out of all this.

That's what I would say to them. Tell them to get some kind of counseling. Maybe where you can have one on one with the person counseling you that you feel comfortable with. They can give you advice as to which services you can use. Just don't try and go it alone. Stick your hand out and ask for help. Don't sit in a shell, and don't dwell on the negative. Try and seek the positive.

Q. What keeps you going these days?

B. I think what keeps me going these days is the belief that the good that I've had in my life can definitely come to me again through all the things that we just discussed. Also, I don't give up easily. There's times when I get into poor me, poor little me, but it's because I'm not doing the things that I'm supposed to do. I've never been someone who gives up. I wouldn't say I'm afraid. I'm not ready to die yet.

Q. What was the last job you had?

B. The last job I had was administrating in a dry-wall company, and helping out in the field. Also, I was in the entertainment business for awhile. I was doing acting and transportation and some stunt work. I was in the business of distribution of natural stone. That was years ago, natural stones like marble and granite for development and interior design. But that's when the alcoholism began to surface. This was probably about eight years ago. I could wake up in the morning and function, but then all of a sudden...

Another piece of advice I have for the homeless, if you do have an addiction with drugs, and you know deep down inside that you are knowledgeable about things in life, and you maybe have had a good education—I came from a very good education, but I had the inability to focus with what was really important in life instead of what I thought or where the next party was or whatever. We all have our strengths. Everybody has something, whether it's compassion for others or what. I'm a people person. I think that's good for the homeless because if you surround yourself with other people, you're going to be able to interact and maybe get in little discussions and find out what problems other people have. It can help you.

Q. Do you have a plan?

B. Yeah, the guy upstairs, my father, my Lord Jesus and my holy spirit is my plan, and I'm letting him steer me the right way instead of Bruce thinking Bruce is the one in charge. But I was born on Easter morning so that kind of puts me in touch with God. You know I feel very fortunate.

(Author's note: Bruce has been a professional surfer for ten years. He has won awards, and has lived in Hawaii and Mexico.)

TOM P.

Tom is a very good looking white man of forty-three. He is six feet tall, and has black hair pulled back into a ponytail, and a well kept black beard. You would not think he was homeless.

Q. Where are you from, Tom?

T. I was born in Evanston, Illinois, near Chicago. But I grew up in Germany. I came here to California twenty-one years ago.

Q. You still have a German accent don't you?

T. (laughs) I'll never lose it!

Q. When did you first become homeless?

T. About seven years ago.

Q. What happened?

T. Well, that's a tricky story. I had my own business for about twelve years. I was getting depressed and overwhelmed at work. I was in the moving business. I was expanding into a big warehouse. That's where it all started. We had about twelve pieces of equipment. We had one tractor, a couple of trailers, a couple of trucks, and a couple of moving vans, and a pick-up truck. We moved into a forty-seven thousand square foot warehouse. We were world wide movers. The way the moving business works is we don't actually have companies in town. Instead of that there are agents which are Local, companies who hook up with major van companies that do most of the interstate hauling.

Anyway, we moved into this big old warehouse and the landlord didn't evict all of the existing tenants. I was being pushed out of my old warehouse, and I had to move in. It was a very crazy time. I had always worked sixty to seventy hours a week, seven days a week. Now I had to try and force the other tenants out.

Q. How did this result in your being homeless?

T. To make this simple, we were regulated by the Public Utilities Commission Department of Transportation, and every quarter you had to file a quarterly return, gross income. So, I forgot to file it one quarter. It can catch up with you. If you don't file a quarterly return they suspend your license. Technically you cannot operate your business after that. They don't give you a warning. Then you just pay a penalty fee, and that takes care of that.

What I didn't know was that after ninety days it's not suspended, it's revoked. You have to file all over again. So that became very tricky. Two years later they caught up with me. I met somebody downtown, somebody there who knew everything about me. Except for a little piece of paper, everything was fine. He just said, "You know, you can just pay a thousand dollar fine and then go through a process." All that paperwork you get, it took about a month or two. In the meantime everybody operates. That was in 1996. I paid him the fine, and then on January 2nd, another lady called. She was in the enforcement branch and had just taken over. She told me to cease and desist. She just came down on me like a pile of bricks.

They can come into your business and go through your files without a warrant. They were looking to make an example of somebody. So they took me to court. It used to be down in Lancaster. There's a whole lot of illegal operators out there who they should chase—operators with Post Office boxes. The case she was trying to make on us was like there was this guy from Lancaster who took people's stuff and loaded it on the truck, got the money up front, and took it to a dump and dumped it. And she was protecting the public from me doing that—to keep me from moving people's stuff out of my warehouse and taking their stuff and be a criminal by dumping their stuff. How preposterous can you get!

After that I got more and more depressed. I did some drinking at that time. She put me out of business. This was about seven years ago. That's how I became homeless. In the process I lost everything. Between her and the landlords, they worked together. He got all my assets, which were worth three to four hundred thousand dollars. I got zero dollars, and I was in bankruptcy. Nothing!

How I first became homeless, they shut off my phones. Then I got evicted. I had some money left, not much. I just was so frustrated about everything. I was in so much pain. I didn't talk to anybody. When I couldn't afford to go to hotels anymore, I started staying in my pick-up truck. That lasted about six months.

Then I stopped drinking. I decided I had to stop buying them. About that time I was getting general delivery at the Post Office. It was very unreliable. In late December of 1997 I got an arraignment notice for December 17th. They charged me for violating the Public Utilities Commission, operating without a license. Now I'm wondering that there's probably a warrant for my arrest.

Anyhow, I stopped drinking and everything. Next thing you know the cops arrested me for some complaint for sleeping behind a furniture store in West L.A. I was in just one night. I had to go to court because of her, and I was fighting with my landlord to release my things. I lost everything in the bankruptcy court. Eventually I got caught up in the court process.

I ended up doing over four months in the county jail for operating without a license. I was very depressed. A psychiatrist cancelled working with me when I got out of jail, and I couldn't get my meds. I didn't know anything about other systems then. I had a couple of friends who I contacted, send me a little money—enough to get some cheap food. Then I came back to Santa Monica and joined Step-Up on Second. (A place that serves people with mental disabilities.) I got out of jail just after election day in 1998 and joined Step-Up in March—just after I got my meds from Edelman. (A Center.)

Q. Where do you sleep?

T. These days I stay on the streets of Santa Monica. I sleep by a Church. I used to spend a lot of time in the park, but I've been having trouble with the police, last year when they beat me anyhow. So now I spend most of my time at Step-Up. I usually come for breakfast and dinner.

Q. Do you have any plans?

T. Actually I'm probably going to go back to Germany. I'm still a European citizen. I can get a house and welfare there. I'll have to get myself over to the consulate to get my passport. So over the next couple of months I'll be doing that. This is not working out, so it's time to make my move. I've got a four year certificate from somewhere you've never heard of before. It's called Feldenkreis. It's a very gentle type of physical therapy. I'm already a therapist. I just have to reinstate my license. It's not accepted by the medical establishment. You have to get people who know about it. I don't know if I'm going to be doing that right away.

Q. Do you have any friends here?

T. Yes, I have a bunch of friends out in the street.

Q. How do you feel about Los Angeles in general?

T. I'm tired of L.A. People have gotten a lot rougher, more aggressive. You used to be able to cross a street at the corner. Now they can run you over. You have to use a pedestrian crosswalk. You're like a rabbit trying to cross Wilshire Boulevard.

Q. How do you spend your days?

T. You know, there's not much to do out there. It's boring. So limited with what you can do with no money. You have to know where you can leave your stuff. I've had my stuff stolen. You stash stuff in the bushes.

Q. What would you say to someone who is new to being homeless?

T. Go to the food lines, hook up with the services. If you have a mental disability, this place (Step-Up) is really helpful. Stay away from the booze and the drugs. If you can go back to work, all the much better.

SCOTT C.

Scott is a white male with shoulder length blond hair. He is sunburned behind sunglasses, and he seems a bit burned out mentally. He is thirty-nine years old.

Q. How long have you been homeless, Scott?

S. I've been homeless kind of off and on for about ten years now. I can get a job. I was living in Wisconsin. My roommate moved out, and then I had to move out. It was in the summer and I started living in my car. I got a ticket for an open container in my car so I lost my car that I was living in. My family was in Wisconsin. When I lost my car I started living in Minnesota in shelters and like that. And then I was staying with my dad for awhile. And then I took a bus to out here.

Q. Why did you come to Los Angeles?

S. I was raised in San Diego, and I don't know. I had a gift that I was going to be a singer. And, I still have it sometimes. Like an angel and a gift you know.

I was born in Wisconsin. I was raised as a child in San Diego. We moved back to Wisconsin when I was seventeen in school. We moved back to Wisconsin where my mom and dad were raised. And then my dad came back to San Diego and my brother did. My mom and dad got a divorce, so we came out here. That was when I was about twenty.

Q. What kind of work have you done?

S. My dad was a carpenter and we did construction work. And then in Wisconsin I had a job at a truck stop. When grandpa retired I worked there and then I got fired. And then I had a gift about ten years ago and I have it sometimes. I'm not sure if I do or not. Me and my dad flew out here two years ago and we got separated. I was hanging around at Venice Beach—sometimes sleeping on the beach, sometimes at the Community Center in the winter—just really doing nothing—laying down on the beach, and Hollywood. I could get a job but I don't know where to go, you know. I work sometimes a little bit. I work at the temporary place. I've worked there maybe one or two days. I get a check that comes every month. (He has been getting SSI for the last fifteen or sixteen years.)

I was working though. In Wisconsin I worked at a truck stop. My dad remarried and came back to Wisconsin. He started doing construction work because he was a carpenter. And I know something about that. I could do that too, but I know I had a gift but don't seem to have it. It's the idea. I can go up to North Hollywood. That's where—that's where—that's where—the way it is now.

Q. What's your view of the world?

S. Now, I don't know for sure. Someone goes around and tells me not to go around, or stay at the beach. I stay on the beach or at the Community Center. I just do whatever I please, actually. I can't remember some things. I drink a lot. I drink mostly. I just got another open container citation. I get them all the time. Go to jail for a couple of days or a month or so.

Q. Have you had any other problems with the Police?

S. Not really. Just some stupid thing that happened down here that I think had been some misunderstanding. Somebody said that I bit a girl. But my memory goes. I don't remember exactly what happened. It was only like a couple of months I was in jail. I don't know how they found me guilty, or not guilty. Usually it's just a few days for tickets.

Q. Are you looking forward to anything?

S. I know I had something to look forward to before, but I don't know anymore if I do or not. You know I can go to the Church, and I was lucky with God before, but now I ain't. Something really didn't work out. I don't really want to try to explain it because I've tried to explain it before to people. I could be lucky and I could be unlucky. I'll do something. I'll probably get married and have children one way or another. I'm thirty-nine you know. I don't have plans you know. I could plan something but I know my past would be better than anything I could get in the future.

Q. You're thirty-nine now. Don't you think having a career as a singer might be out of reach?

S. You don't know God! If you knew God you'd know (laughs).

I know I do. Anybody that I talk to, they think they know Him but they don't. I don't want to say it, but I see. I know Jesus. As we speak I can see Him. But you don't see Him (laughs). But it's the truth. He comes into my head and I can see Him in the sky. Me, I could feel some calmness in my surrounding. And I had a gift you know. You can either have it or not have it. People who don't know wouldn't understand anyway. If you know what your life is then you know yourself. My father was a carpenter, and my brother worked for Anderson windows.

Q. Are you planning on going back to these same jobs?

S. That's what I'll do. I'll get a job right now. I should be working anyways. I know that I'll get that one check that I got before. I get it and then I get drunk and screw around. And then—screw around. With God you can win or lose. It's either win, or lose. I know you've heard other stories but I bet they don't know God. I know God.

MARIA H.

I interviewed Maria at the Union Rescue Mission in Los Angeles. She is Hispanic, about 5'6" with long brown hair and brown eyes. She has two children who were with her at the time of the interview. A baby girl was in a carriage and her little boy clung to her legs throughout our talk.

Q. How old are your children?
M. Matthew is two and Brenda is one.
Q. Are you from Los Angeles originally?
M. No, I'm from El Paso, Texas.
Q. How did you find yourself in Los Angeles?
M. Well, I heard there were a lot of jobs here. I've been trying to get a job for months.
Q. How old are you?
M. I am thirty-eight.
Q. Why are you homeless?
M. They were renovating the apartment, and I had no place to go.
Q. How long have you been at the Rescue Mission?
M. Two to three months.
Q. How do you take care of the children?
M. They stay with me. We have hot meals three times a day. They have a bed. I get clothing. I get to shower with my children. I have access to laundry machines on the next street.
Q. Do you get GR?
M. No, I get welfare for the children.
Q. Are you looking for work now?
M. I have been looking for a child care job or something like that where I can start working. It's hard because the child care jobs around here are taken.
Q. How is it living at the shelter?
M. It's great. You get to shower and get clothes and meals. During the day I am with my kids.
Q. How much do you get from Welfare?
M. About five hundred a month.
Q. Have you ever had to go to a doctor?
M. Yes, I have. I have Medi-Cal for the babies only. They treat them for colds.
Q. Have you had any troubles with other people here at the Mission?

M. No. Everything is pretty cool. You just mind your own business. Everybody minds their own business. I'm waiting for an apartment now, but first I have to find work.

Q. What has your education been?

M. I had some college. I have a High School GED. I went to a community college. I had about a semester going there, but at the same time I was working and I just could not keep this up. It's very hard to go to work and go to school at the same time.

FREDERICK

Frederick is a white man about six feet, one. He is fifty-four years old, and speaks in a low tone.

Q. Where are you from?

F. I'm from Los Angeles.

Q. Tell me about your childhood.

F. Ummm, how would I describe it? Almost idyllic. I came from a very nice family. Had loads of love. I can't remember my parents once raising their hand to me.

Q. What about your education?

F. I've been through Graduate school.

Q. Did you finish Graduate school?

F. No. ABT, all but thesis. I was writing a thesis for the department of Anthropology. I had met a girl and got married. Our marriage broke up at that time. We had been touring the world for a couple of years. Backpacks, like that. We had been together eight or nine years.

Q. How long have you been homeless?

F. Off and on since 1994.

Q. What led to your being homeless?

F. I ran out of money. Money from the property that I sold, ran out. I did not pay the death taxes to the IRS on my parents' estate. I had about ten thousand in my account which the IRS confiscated.

Q. How did you feel at the time?

F. I really don't know. I'd—I was a little bit astounded, but not surprisingly I was in probate myself.

Q. How did you feel about living outside?

F. I've been a backpacker all of my life. I kept my backpack and my hiking boots. Hit the outdoors, applied for GR. SSI is not a likely prospect.

Q. Where do you get food?

F. I buy my own.

Q. With GR?

F. With GR.

Q. You have enough to get you through?

F. Oh yeah. Just so much for budgeting a day. I even have some left over at the end of the month.

Q. How about your clothing?

F. I buy them at the thrift shop down the street.

Q. Where are you sleeping?

F. In doorways that do not have "No sitting" signs. So during inclement weather I always seek out doorways that I can stay in, and there have been quite a few.

Q. Do you panhandle?

F. No, I have no need.

Q. What's a typical day for you?

F. I spend the bulk of the week, Monday through Friday, I go down to the St. Joseph Center in Venice. And generally I walk around. I read books at the library. I have ceased looking for work. I call some friends, I occasionally go out. I guess on a typical day I spend a lot of time in various libraries reading.

Q. Have you ever had to physically protect yourself?

F. Uh huh. I got hit (laughs). I was hit over the head by a twenty-four ounce bottle of beer by someone passing by. This was some years ago. I woke up in the emergency room. I had something happen just the other day outside of the library. Some guy came up and said, "Are you a pirate?" A young guy, kind of disheveled looking. I said, "I beg your pardon." And then he hit me and then walked off.

Q. What about the Police? Any problems with them?

F. I would not say I had any problems with the Police. They've taken me into custody. Once I was drunk as a skunk. They took me in and released me in a couple of hours.

I had done a little experimenting on them. I wanted to see how this was going to be judicated. I got several tickets for sleeping in a doorway, and I deliberately let them go to warrant. I kept sleeping in the same doorway. They came up and asked me did I have any warrants, and I said, "I hope so, I've been trying to get them." They took me into city jail, transferred me to LA county jail. I went through the process from there. As soon as the process was finished they began to process me out and release me. That's how I found out that's how they judicate ticket warrants—in an experiment. Curiosity satisfied.

Q. Are you worried about anything?

F. I worry about getting hit again. I do suffer from stress, and I'm getting tired. The impact of long term emotional stress is typical to living this kind of life.

Q. Do you have any dreams as to what you would like to be doing?

F. Well, I really wouldn't call them dreams. I would like to work in the human service sector; in the field of mental health and psychiatry, and social services.

Q. Do you get bored?

F. Very bored! I think I've read more books in the last eight or nine years than I ever did as an under-graduate student.

Q. Have you had any girlfriends while you've been homeless?

F. Shall we say they seem to have some obvious emotional problems, these homeless women. I do have a girlfriend in Glendora. She works as a travel agent.

Q. Do you have friends?

F. Many. I have three or four friends I would consider very close to me. I know a great many people here and in Glendora. I am friendly with some case managers at St. Josephs.

Q. How do you view the world in general?

F. Fundamentally unchanged. Depending on what region of the world in which you live, it can be very dangerous. The world seems to be getting more dangerous—for Americans anyway.

DAVID R.

David is a full blooded, native American Indian. He is 5'11" and has a graying moustache. He is fifty-four years old.

Q. Where are you from originally?

D. Anadark, Oklahoma.

Q. Were you homeless in Oklahoma?

D. Yes. I had no money so I got on the street. I've stayed in shelters and lived on the street. I applied for SSI. It took me six months to get it. When I got SSI it really wasn't enough money to do anything with so I remained on the street. Now I'm a vet and I get even more money, but I'm still on the street because it's not enough to get a place.

Q. When were you in the service?

D. Long before I was homeless. I was in the Marines.

Q. What was your childhood like?

D. I was a very abused child. My father is an alcoholic and my grandfather was an alcoholic. I'm a recovering alcoholic myself.

Q. Are you on a twelve step program?

D. Nope. But I do the twelve steps, 'cause I'm still clean and sober.

Q. How did you do in school?

D. I graduated high school and went through one year of college.

Q. Where are you staying?

D. Right now, at Venice Beach.

Q. Do you sleep on the beach?

D. I usually sleep on the grass out in the park.

Q. What are you doing for clothing?

D. This pair of pants, socks, two T-shirts, and a coat are my only clothes at the moment.

Q. How long has it been since you stopped getting SSI?

D. It's been fifteen years. I'm a Vietnam vet, and I get a service connected pension from the Marines. It helps me get by somewhat. I haven't got enough money so I can get into a place yet.

Q. How much do you get?

D. A little over $800.00.

Q. Do you panhandle at all?

D. Nope. That's something I refuse to do, asking people for money.

Q. What do you do all day?

D. Ah, waking up, sometimes take a shower, change clothes if I have some new clothes, and go find something to do until it's time to go to bed. I walk around. I go to Venice Beach. I help people sell stuff. I make runs to the store for them. They don't want to leave their area so I go to the store for them. I write poetry.

Q. Have you had any trouble with the Police?

D. Nope. I got one ticket since I've been out here. I've been out here for about twelve days. I came here from Long Beach. The Police are nasty there. I was there for five or six months. The Police harass you very hard. Give you a ticket for camping out anywhere, sleeping out anywhere except the shelter, and I don't do shelters. I'm trying to get off the street.

Q. What keeps you from getting off the street?

D. Not enough money.

Q. How come you've been homeless for so long?

D. Well, every time I get to a situation to where I can get into something there's always a bunch of money up front.

I did something this morning I haven't done for a long time is going over to Starbucks to see if I could get enough money to get a cup of coffee and sit there and charge my telephone because a lady bought me one. I couldn't even panhandle me up a dollar and fifty cents. That's pretty nasty. I had to go in there looking like I was reading the paper and do it anyway.

Q. Have you ever had to steal?

D. Nope.

Q. What is your last name?

D. Red Feather. My middle name is Two Eagles.

Q. Tell me about your education.

D. I graduated High School in 1966. I went to a specialty college and became a certified welder, and I haven't used any of it since.

Q. Do you have any friends out here?

D. Very few. They're just as homeless as I am, and they always ask for money so I stay away from 'em. I don't like to panhandle unless I absolutely have to.

Q. Do you have any advice for anyone who has just become homeless?

D. Well, if you can work, work. If you can't, take advantage of what you find. Can you show me the book you're writing? (I showed him the work in progress.) I'd read it. I think it would be interesting.

GARY P.

Gary is Caucasian, about 5'9" with shoulder length brown hair with touches of grey. He is fifty-four years old.

Q. How long have you been homeless, Gary?

G. To give you the best estimate, my last apartment was either in San Diego in 1979 or in Norwich Connecticut in 1975. As far as being a legalized tenant, I was homeless. In 1979 I'm not sure the landlord had paperwork signed by me or not. I can offer you a little information here. I robbed a bank and got away with it that year. There has been some success in my psychological aptitude. This was in San Diego in 1979.

Q. So, it's okay to write about this?

G. Legally, yes.

Q. How interesting.

G. (laughs) You might say that, since I was delivered by Doc Holiday.

Q. What kind of schooling have you had?

G. I think I completed the ninth grade. That was in Norwich, Connecticut, the home of Benedict Arnold. I did average in school, about a C plus.

Q. Where are you getting your food?

G. From a dumpster behind a market in Trancas. I'm living on the side of a small mountain.

Q. Where do you get your clothes?

G. I find them.

Q. Where do you get cleaned up?

G. I don't have a certain spot or place that I go to. I'm able to stay relatively clean within the behavior activity that I exhibit. I don't orientate to a certain place.

Q. You go awhile between showers.

G. I think you could say that.

Q. Do you get SSI or GR?

G. I get a direct deposit, electronic deposit from the government (SSI) of eight hundred and seventy-two dollars.

Q. How long have you been getting it?

G. Five years. I did have it before in '72 for my complicity in Water Gate. Fiasco, breakage. I was on Social Security for a year while doing Federal parole.

Q. Do you panhandle?

G. Yes. As a matter of fact I was in court today for aggressive panhandling. I have a continuance until the eighth of April. At which time I will be offered the opportunity to elect a jury or go to trial for the alleged offense. It's a companion case.

There was a fellow who was homeless with me about a year ago who was sitting with me while I was on parole. He alleges, and I have read some of his motions. Because of some heroin, he was given about five to seven years.

Q. What was the outcome?

G. I don't know because I am in a sort of harassment state of affairs. In my opinion I have been harassed by the Police. As things go, day by day, I can only tell you that I'm playing things by ear. I just thought you might be interested. I did have an extensive record.

Q. Why have you been homeless all this time?

G. That's a very good question. I think I've been homeless for this long because of a large amount of reason, which would require me to spend much more time today than you're able to spend with me, to explain to your satisfaction. How a messianic psychological state can be manipulated and personally victimized for years by my family and friends. I've been homeless for this long for that reason. And also, I think it's just come a time for this civilization in America, where we live, you and I, to stop the landlord frenzy and to do the best that I can to be a man of ideals, and not support that element regardless if I'm able to or not—a fanatical or moral or political point of view. I just have strong feelings as you can tell, that that element, the landlord/client relationship is poor.

You know, you try. I had a small settlement from the Academy Awards when I fell off the roof and injured my left foot, thirty-two thousand, around there. And it was an opportunity for me then in Florida to put a foot in the ground, to put a mailbox there. Have something tangible. I was used and manipulated at that place in time because of my ineptitude perhaps. I don't know if that word is descriptive enough. My last name is Phrades, from the Euphrades river.

Q. Have you had a girlfriend?

G. I met the girl of my dreams. I was very much interested in pursuing a lady named Joy. Raise you right hand by God, and check behind your back. Her and I are still a hot item. At that time I was deprived of opportunity in this country because I believe that the money I had captured wasn't progressive money. My father who had polio in his left arm, as they say the Kaiser had, said to me, "If there's no progress, what's the sense of going on?" He said I shouldn't have any animosity towards Florida, but that's just the way things are in life.

I became disillusioned, I guess, so money became meaningless. In fact I couldn't wait to see the end of it. I wanted to get back to work to demonstrate my ability to survive. I actually did get back to work.

Q. What kind of work?

G. Some odds and ends work, part time tradesman stuff. I put a trailer park in for Wilma. That's a woman in Alabama. I spent three years constructing her field of dreams. I got a little bit of work, and it did help me some. I don't hate her for using my time up, and we are friends today. But it cost severely.

You know I was delivered by Doc Holiday, March the sixth, 1950, in westerly Rhode Island. It seems to me that every thing that's going on with me is Freudian. I guess that would be the best way to describe it. The most primitive and basic talents that they have. There's very little freedom to me.

Q. Is there anything you enjoy doing?

G. I do enjoy going down to Mexico because they're behind us, anatomically, religiously, biologically. That to me, that's an interesting place. I am well respected and regarded there. I know enough Spanish after twenty years not to take a dishwashing job.

VALERIE

Valerie is a forty-three year old black woman, petite, about 5'4". Her black hair falls just below her shoulders, and she is wearing a white summer hat and an African dress with a large silver crucifix around her neck. She is attractive, uses make-up sparingly, and is very easy to converse with. She carries her home with her—a rolling suitcase and three large bags.

Q. How long have you been homeless?

V. I have been homeless at least five years. I'm looking for a different kind of house.

Q. Where are you from?

V. I was born in New York City, but I had been staying in San Francisco.

Q. Are you going back to San Francisco?

V. Yes, my doctor is there. For a doctor here I go to the Veterans Administration.

Q. Were you in the service?

V. No. My father was.

Q. Why did you become homeless?

V. Well, Santa Monica doesn't have a shelter. It keeps people moving around from one place to another. People think homeless people look like we're all on drugs or bad people, or people who want to go to jail. That's not true. The history of this country is about being free to move. You can't change the system when you want to be somewhere else. So I have to go along with what they're doing here.

I'm not the Mayor of Santa Monica. They say they don't have a shelter, and you can't afford a hotel. You don't have to spend your money at a hotel. You can get a blanket and go to the beach and enjoy yourself. Instead of saying these are good people in transition who aren't bothering anybody—some looking for work and housing or something.

Q. Tell me a little about your family.

V. I was born in New York. Most of my family lives in Philadelphia. Philadelphia and Virginia and North and South Carolina. I do have relatives in California but not my parents.

Q. What caused you to become transient in the first place?

V. I like to travel. I love to travel. So being transient, or whatever they call it, doesn't bother me.

Q. Where are some places you've been?

V. One thing I've been able to do is see the United States, which most people take for granted. Say you want to go to Florida—most people haven't had the opportunity to appreciate how beautiful this country is. Not even Californians. People that have stayed in Los Angeles who have transportation jobs, you ask them "ever been to Santa Barbara?" They say oh, no.

Q. Where are you getting your meals?

V. I go to Daybreak when I'm not out here. I go there every other day. If not Daybreak you can go to the Salvation Army and get a bag lunch.

Q. Have you been making any money now that you're out here?

V. I get a check from the Veterans Administration. It's called Benefits for the children of Veterans. I'm listed as a dependent. And I'm grateful that I can use that and take some time off. I've worked all my life since I was very young. I have worked as a teacher for youngsters. So I stayed in that kind of work.

Q. What do you do during the day?

V. Well, I sleep with a very nice group of people. I do have a schedule of appointments when I came here. But, when I don't have any appointments I just hang out and talk to people. See what everybody's doing. It's like are we making progress or are we all just standing still. That's why I like the coffee shop. Places where you can catch people and talk. It makes me so upset that McDonalds down the street discriminates against homeless people. When people are hungry or needs a cigarette, they can't hang around there. But you can tell them to go to the Salvation Army. A lot of people congregate there.

Q. Have you any problems with the Police?

V. I wouldn't call it a problem, but I wasn't really happy until I got to know them and how they work. When they become familiar with you, then you can begin to communicate with them.

Q. Have you gotten tickets?

V. Yes I have, jaywalking. I got one ticket that I couldn't believe 'cause I crossed the street with a thousand other people and I asked "why are you picking on me?" We, everybody, crosses there but it's still against the law.

Q. How did you pay the ticket?

V. I went over to the ticket desk you know, where you sign up to go to court. That ticket I just paid it, 'cause it was only ten dollars, and I was on my way back up north and I didn't want to come back and go to court, so I just ate it. But I should have gone to court with the ticket. I also got a ticket for an open container. I had bought a beer in Venice. I took a sip out of it, put it back in my bag for lunch time. I had it in my shopping bag with my lunch in it. I put the beer in there. When I got back in Santa Monica at the pier, the Police Officer followed over here. And real funny he said, "Where's the beer?" I said, "What, do you have X-ray vision or something?" Because he had followed me. That ticket was three hundred and something dollars. I went to court. The Judge gives you a choice about how to resolve the ticket.

Q. Did you have to do community service?

V. I didn't do community service. I did something else. The Judge told me, "This is my court and it is a very crowded place." I paid the court fee just for showing up, which wasn't bad. I paid about twenty dollars. I really wasn't drinking it. What did I do that was so terrible?

Q. Do you have any worries?

V. You mean as a homeless person? My biggest worry is to be deciding who I want to be. If I decide to stay in this area here, where do I want to be? I'm not really sure where I want to live. I don't want to tie myself down. I'd like to work three days a week.

We have rights! I mean it sounds kind of corny, but start to pay attention to what's happening on television and the newspapers. Politicians are really fired up because in this country it's a constant loss of rights. We have rights. Like I want to put a support group together. Well, these places that they have they want to talk to you about your SSI, what kind of diagnoses you have. That's not relevant to me.

People need to look at everybody as equal. I will treat you as a man and I'm a woman. I know people who work every day. They got homes, children, cars, bank accounts, save money, buy food, but it's the same thing we do every day. It's not different. But when you sit down and talk to a lot of professional people they talk to you like you're something different. And we're not different. We have the right to say where we want to go and what we want to do.

We're losing that right to privacy. We need a support group that we can just talk with ourselves as just people. It's really spooky. If you leave somebody out on that street, they will change and become so cold. It's enough to make you cry. And you say what the hell happened to Robert? I see it every day.

How do you go to these programs and nobody helps you to get a check? I don't know what these people are doing. White and black people, mostly white, like a woman, why do you want to beg somebody for a cigarette, when you go to this place and that place every day.

Q. Sometimes people think that you're a cigarette machine.

V. Well, you know how a pack of cigarettes will go. I mean how can a person do without a welfare check? All you have to say is "This is the address, and here's two bus tokens, and go get your check and food stamps." I do it all the time. It's gotten to be such a cold world. It's a shame how they treat the homeless people. So cold. Cause we want to have sex, eat good food, just like anybody else.

PAUL S.

Paul is a Caucasian male about 5'9". He wears a beanie cap over waist-long red hair, and has a close cut beard. He is twenty-eight years old.

Q. Where did you grow up?

P. New Haven, Connecticut. My parents were divorced, and I lived with my dad.

Q. When did you come out to California?

P. About four or five years ago.

Q. Have you been homeless since you've been here?

P. No, I just been homeless for the past two years.

Q. What happened?

P. I lost my job. I was working at a Video distributor. Companies would give us videos and we would distribute them to different stores.

Q. Why did you lose your job?

P. They, unh—when Bush went into office, there was an indictment against the place I worked. So they went out of business. I was already in the red working there. It was like a job that I'd do before I got a job that I really wanted. I was barely paying the rent and they were barely paying me.

Q. What kept you from getting another job?

P. Well, I got evicted from my place 'cause I was two months behind in rent. The landlord found out that I lost my job. Periodically I'll work through Labor Ready or stuff like that.

Q. What kind of work have you done for them?

P. Data entry, and warehouse stuff too.

Q. How did you feel when you first became homeless?

P. When this initially happened I was staying with friends, sleeping on couches and stuff like that. And I did that for a few months. I would do that, and then sometimes I would stay out, or sometimes I would get a hotel room. I was already in debt. I couldn't stay at these places indefinitely. I went on GR the first year, and I haven't got back on it for a year.

Q. How are you eating?

P. The Churches. They have a place to shower and clean up. All that stuff you have to do in the afternoon. So when I do go to an employment office, it's like I have to get a late interview with them. It's not like I can go there the first thing in the morning. There's like a hundred people who need showers.

Q. Where are you staying now?

P. On the beach.

Q. Do you panhandle at all?

P. No. I don't want to be among the hundreds of people doing it.

Q. What do you do during the day?

P. I spend a lot of time at the library. I've been preparing a resume to try to get back to work. I've been debating whether or not to put I was homeless in the resume.

Q. Have you ever had to protect yourself out on the streets?

P. Just chasing people who steal my stuff. I've been in a few altercations that have bordered on violence, just shouting, but not really out there.

Q. Any tickets?

P. I got one ticket for Jay walking. Actually they just wanted to stop me and talk to me. You know what I mean? I went to court and it got dismissed.

Q. Have you had any medical visits while you've been out here?

P. Well, that's the next thing I'm going to do. I just need to get a physical because it's so long since I've had one. There are places that will do that for you. I have like—somebody hit me in the head—I think the term is called tinnitus, where there is a ringing in your ears. So periodically there is ringing in my ears. And I know that's a specialized doctor who will take care of that. There's probably nothing they can do. It's more like it's something that I'm going to have the rest of my life. I don't know.

Q. What would you like to be doing?

P. I'd like to be making money. Yeah. You need money to have money.

Q. You look clean enough to get a job. Why can't you?

P. This is me at my absolute worst. And I do work. I mean I've done extra work. Whenever I have money I will stay at a hotel for several nights. Then once that's gone, you know what I mean? You have several hundred dollars. You can rent a place for several months. And if you're working, you feel stupid not spending the money, you know what I mean? Like if you're saving your money and working and being homeless, I mean that's the stupidest thing in the world, to save it while you're homeless.

The thing about working at the warehouse is you have to be there at five o'clock in the morning, and transportation and that whole thing. It's like you're working eight hours, but it's really twelve hours out of your day. And the fact that you're homeless, you never relax. So I don't do that much. I mean there are people doing it and they kill themselves doing it. Sometimes they'll live in their car.

Q. So what kind of work would you like to be doing?

P. I have no idea. In my work history everything I've done has been graphics, radio or entertainment type stuff. So that's what I'm trained to do. So jumping into that after being out of work for two or two and a half years, it's almost impossible. And to get there, it's really about a three or four hour thing to get cleaned up and get a meal. It takes forever to do. I know that a lot people here think they're taking care of the homeless, but they're not. You can't live in a country and not feed the citizens. Especially now—the way it is with this administration.

Q. What kind of an education do you have?

P. I have a degree in graphics. I went to the Design Center. It's like an Art school.

Q. What would you tell someone who is newly homeless?

P. I don't know what I'd say to a person who is homeless. A lot of people are homeless because of drugs. I'd say most of them are homeless because of drugs. So, you know what I mean? I don't associate with people for the most part.

Q. Is that kind of lonely?

P. Yes. Seems like everyone has a chemical dependency. I don't know how many people here you talked to. There are some people out here who are educated and smart. For them, they fouled it up because of drugs. If I was ever going to start taking drugs it would be now. I'm not into it.

Q. What is your view of the world right now?

P. Well, this country is about to fall apart economically. I've traveled across the western part of the United States. It just took a few months, and I did it fairly recently. Out here the country really doesn't represent the way the country actually is. The country is really, really, really sinking. And the places that are wealthy like here or wherever, I think are sucking resources away from the rest of the country.

This state's already about to go bankrupt, and we're doing better than most of the country. That is reality. I mean our gross national product, because we're so gigantic, this country's like a dinosaur. It's huge, but it's just lumbering along. It's not going anywhere. A lot of people who are wealthy, they should be wealthier. I don't have a problem with rich people. But a lot of them are getting ripped off.

Q. Maybe you should be a politician.

P. I really don't like dealing with people. I wouldn't want the responsibility. To be honest with you, I really don't like homeless people. I have a hard time telling if their problems are the results of their situation or the cause of their situation. I've met people who have really, really drank a lot. I think maybe if they were doing better, then they wouldn't be under stress and their drinking would improve. But, I don't drink so…

Q. What do you do during the day?

P. I go to the library. I'll think about stuff. Also I have my plan for as soon as I'm not homeless. I have a plan of everything I'm going to do, and everything that has to be done. I do research on things that interest me, and that are relevant. It's real complicated.

I want to see a doctor about my fatigue. 'Cause when you're homeless, I'm sure my immune system, fatigue starts to break me down little by little. I used to be really, really, really athletic. And it's the most unhealthy thing in the world to be homeless. The elements, everything, are just constantly, constantly destroying you. If I worked at not making a lot of money, all I would be doing is going month to month, which is where I was before. If you hit a snag, there's no net. And so it really doesn't motivate me to do that.

I work when it's necessary. The people who earn month to month pay and manage is because they have a family and a community thing. I've lived with roommates, and I'm tired of living with roommates. There's one person I talked to as far as living as roommates, but he drinks too much.

You know, the President wants people to be homeless so he can put them in prison. Most of the prisons are built by private companies. They are trying to squeeze everybody out. I was never homeless my whole life until we've had this president. All of a sudden I'm homeless. It's impossible to get a place. It wasn't always like that. He wants people out in the streets, and like he wants to open up the borders. If you look at it on paper, he looks like a Nazi. He wants to get rid of Section 8 (low cost government subsidized housing), and in his words, "faith based initiatives", Churches to take care of people. He's going to lose the election, and then he's probably going to go to prison.

KAZ M.

Kaz is a 6'3" black male with a dreadlock hair style. He is twenty-five years old.

Q. How long have you been on the street?
K. Three or four months.
Q. Why did you become homeless?
K. I relocated. I came back to California from North Carolina.
Q. Were you born in California?
K. Yes.
Q. Did you have a place to stay in North Carolina?
K. Yes.
Q. Why did you move back?
K. It was just my twenty-fifth birthday.
Q. Is this the first time you have been homeless?
K. Yup.
Q. How do you feel being homeless?
K. It's cool. I like it.
Q. Where are you staying?
K. I'm sleeping in the parking structure.
Q. Where are you getting your food?
K. GR and food lines.
Q. What do you do about clothing?
K. People buy me clothes.
Q. Is GR all you get?
K. My parents are helping me out a little bit. And people offer me food.
Q. Have you panhandled?
K. No.
Q. What do you do during the day?
K. Hang out. Go to the bookstore or library. Smoke a joint. That's pretty much my day. Reading, soda, and hanging out with my friends.
Q. Any problems with the Police since you've been back?
K. I got a ticket for sitting in the parking structure. And the other day they were asking me who I was. They took my information. I have friends that didn't have I.D. and they've been arrested about three times.
Q. What kind of education have you had?
K. About three years of college. I studied theater.
Q. Are you an actor?

K. I guess I'm an actor. I write and direct, too. Pretty much I'm working at rewriting my screenplay. Also, other treatments as they come to me. Pretty much not doing anything. I pride myself on that. It's like how cool is it just to be happy and not have to do anything.

Q. Do you want to tell me your story?

K. Well, this whole thing is interesting because when I first came out here I was staying with my God parents. And then I had to leave there 'cause the holidays were coming. And so I was doing a lot of reading and meditation, and a lot of spiritual work. I had gotten to this cross roads in my work. It's like, don't ask for anything from man. Ask for everything from God. Or, understand that all your needs will be met at the universe as source. Not to go to man.

Basically, what that meant to me was in my situation was not to ask anybody for a place to stay at their house. And so I just kinda came out on the street. I came with the clothes that I felt comfortable carrying, and no money really, and a book. And, I'm just sitting there on the promenade, reading my book, constantly reaffirming to myself that the universe is my source, and God will supply me with everything I need.

So like a day into it, somebody comes up to me as I'm sitting on the bench reading, and they bring me a blanket and socks and a sandwich. I just looked at them, and that's when I kind of understood. A lot of stuff really made sense to me. I could see everybody around me and everything in my life is a gift from God. I can look at these people and see them as blessings, as true gifts straight from God. I learned a lot from that. God is so abundant in my life. In these last three months it's constantly that thing that keeps unfolding.

There was one other time in the last three months that I've had to realize that God is my source and that the universe is my source. In three quarters of the day, the same thing happened, almost the exact same circumstances. I was reading. The key thing about these circumstances is that I didn't do anything. I'm walking down the street, reading a book, and these people actually pass me, and then they turned around, they get my attention and asked, "Would you like something to eat?"

From that point I've been going deeper and deeper, really getting into like interesting stuff, like the Christ stuff, of manhood and stuff, that every man has the potential to be Jesus Christ.

Q. Was that something that you discovered, or was it something that was written?

K. It was written. Like, I've wrestled with it. I've looked at it, and like being out here there has been numerous situations where I've run into people who don't agree with me, and contradictory beliefs.

First of all, I don't have a religion. I'm not a Christian, so I can look at Jesus Christ the same way as I can look at Buddha, Krishna, and numerous other people who have reached enlightenment. You know—the Pope, Ralph Waldo Emerson, people who have reached enlightenment in the path of manhood. Once you're enlightened, you evolve into a being of light, no longer having a need for your body.

I don't believe in death. I believe in versions of Heaven and Hell. Heaven is here and now, and Hell, however you see the world, and do you believe it or not. Your eyes determine what you see. I live in a perfect world. I live in Eden and Utopia presently. And in moments of discord in my life, it's just a challenge in furthering, opening up that place.

Q. What do you see yourself doing in the near future?

K. Being a movie extra. They call you in every day, various places. You make fifty bucks a day. I'll do that until I get a place or just somewhere that I can shower regularly. I've got a job lined up waiting tables in Venice. A friend of mine's friend owns a restaurant.

Q. Are you still going to do anything with your art?

K. Definitely. As soon as possible I'm going to take some classes at the UCLA extension for directing, editing, and stuff like that. I've got such a backlog of ideas. I've got a ten minute script written. I've got documentary treatments pretty much laid out, video possibilities—my emphasis for coming out here. I'm into astrology and numerology. My numerology says that this is an eight year, a year of gaining, and getting a lot. So, I'd rather do that in Los Angeles than in North Carolina. It's a bigger market, more energy.

I've gained so much that I never expected to gain. I've gained peace of mind that holds no weight for me anymore. My art form has just become a way to glorify God. I want to share my love of God.

JAMES X.

James is a Caucasian male about 6'2". He has short almost black hair. He is wearing a daisy on his ear. He is twenty-four years old. He is carrying a very long skateboard.

Q. Tell me about your skateboard.

J. I found it in the trash can, a dumpster, when I was just out there seeing what I could find. I'm working on it. I just got the hardware together. Before when I'd get down to the bottom of the hill I would have to tighten up the bolts. It works good now.

Q. Where are you originally from?

J. I was born out in Apple Valley, California. My mother died when I was five years old. She died on her birthday. There was a birthday party for her and she never showed up. My dad was in a Veterans home. I never really knew him. I lived at my grandmother's. When I was seventeen they sent me to Washington to live with my dad, but he was living in a truck. So I lived with him a little while and I ended up going to Portland. I hitchhiked there. I lived there on the streets for a couple of months. I got a Greyhound bus to Southern California to my grandmother's. Then she passed away. I couldn't handle it, so I just left and came out here to Santa Monica.

I been out here about a year. At first I hitchhiked and went back to Portland. I ended up leaving. Some people were in a van and they were headed down to Venice so I jumped in with them. They dropped me off in Venice and they said they'd be back in two days to go back to Portland, but they never showed up. I just ended up wandering and living on the beach for awhile. So I moved up into the park. From the park to the alleys. Then I was in downtown LA living in the tunnels, doing whatever I could. I've been homeless about a year.

Q. How do you get your food?

J. Sometimes I go recycling. Sometimes I eat out of the trash can, like behind Jack-In-The-Box. People sometimes give me change but I spend that on alcohol. Now I've been sober for almost three months. I just got out of County jail.

Q. What were you in jail for?

J. Being under the influence.

Q. Of what?

J. Dope, speed. I'm more of an alcoholic myself. The liquor store is about as far as I make it.

Q. How long were you in jail?

J. I did a "county year"—that was forty-two days. Just last Friday I was smoking a cigarette and the cops came up and arrested me. I had a warrant or something. There shouldn't have been a warrant since I served my time and got into a program and all that. I go for drug counseling and Alcoholics Anonymous. I haven't actually started AA yet. When I was in jail they put me in the padded room. This was three days this time.

Q. When you lived with your grandmother, what kind of childhood did you have?

J. It was a good childhood. I had a lot of friends. We lived on a little ranch. It had cows and animals and ducks and stuff. There were motorcycles. We'd go four-wheeling out in the desert. Then when I was a little older I started drinking. We'd get kegs and just sit around a bonfire drinking. We had the garage fixed up for music. We had lights and everything. We would party and stuff. I couldn't find any work out there so I came out here. I still haven't found any work. I almost got a job at Ralph's, but I didn't have a phone and it was hard going in there every day. It was too far.

Q. Do you get GR?

J. I went to Social Services when I got out of jail. They put me on disability. I can go to Edelman and the Venice Family Clinic. I get sixty dollars in food stamps. I get GR too.

Q. Do you panhandle?

J. I used to panhandle a lot more before I got GR. Now I just panhandle for a beer once in awhile. I say "Donations for the cause—'cause I need a forty." As you know I'm not supposed to be drinking. I haven't had a drink in three months—just a beer once in awhile. I'm all clean right now. I just got out of County.

Q. Where did you get your clothes?

J. I found these pants just walking down the street. I found the pants, my T-shirt. The boxers I stole from jail.

Q. What do you do with yourself during the day?

J. I ride around and hope I'll find something in an alley or a dumpster. I find video tapes and DVD's that I can take to the record stores and get a couple of bucks. I also do art but it's too hard to get art supplies. I like to do paintings. Just abstracts. I've been doing that all my life.

I also do calligraphy. I went to school and majored in Philosophy but I didn't have enough money to buy the book. I was going to Community College. I had one semester. They say everybody gets a chance you know. I've been trying to get Section 8 but I'm thinking it would be strange to be inside again.

Q. What about the Police? Any problems?

J. Well, I got arrested for smoking in the park. I lit up a cigarette and two cars swarmed me.

Q. Have you had to see a doctor?

J. I got a staph infection. There's a big lawsuit going but I really haven't had time to find a lawyer. Somebody told me about it. I had one on my neck and one on my back. Really horrible. I really don't want to be around lawyers or court houses.

Q. Is there anything that you would like to be?

J. I always wanted to be an aeronautical engineer. Design airplanes. My mom wanted me to be an astronaut. When I was a little kid there was the Columbia out there in Edwards Air Force base. That was pretty cool. That takes a lot of school. I'd have to join the army or something like that. But I think it's a little late. I'm twenty-six now. I went down to San Diego when I was seventeen to join the Marines. It was for delayed entry for any field I wanted to go in. I wasn't really into it.

Q. Have you ever had to steal before?

J. No, I'm not a thief.

Q. Any girlfriends?

J. There was one chick in downtown LA, but I really wouldn't call her a girlfriend, just a friend.

Q. What is your perspective on the world?

J. From my perspective, I'm God and everybody in their house is hiding. I'm not scared of the street. I don't mind being out on the street. That's what hip-hop is all about.

LENNEA

Lennea is a young Caucasian girl of eighteen. She has long, light brown hair. She rode over on a skateboard.

Q. How long have you been riding a skateboard?

L. Since I was eleven.

Q. Where are you from?

L. I was born in Santa Cruz. I been in Los Angeles four months.

Q. How long have you been homeless?

L. Four months. I got evicted from my place in Oregon. I was working at a ski resort.

Q. Is this the first time you've been in Southern California?

L. Yes.

Q. How did you lose your job in Oregon?

L. I quit.

Q. How was your childhood?

L. It was all right. I lived with my dad. I then lived with my mom when I was thirteen. They divorced when I was eight.

Q. How did you do in school?

L. I graduated High School. I'm going to try to get a place so that I can go back to school. I've been applying for jobs, but it's hard to find work.

Q. Were you frightened when you became homeless?

L. No, I was living down here with my boyfriend. I have a black boyfriend. He's in jail now. I stay with my friends. I know who are my friends now. People like to try to take advantage of me all the time. All my friends look out for me. I can sleep the whole night without people trying to wake me up to ball me.

Q. Where are you getting fed?

L. Anywhere. OPCC (Ocean Park Community Center). I'm trying to get GR and food stamps, but I have to deal with the Oregon employment office. I need to prove that I'm not employed. I got a food stamp card but they won't activate it. I'm doing mail tag with Oregon.

Q. Do you panhandle?

L. Not really. But you can make money real fast that way as a girl.

Q. What is your boyfriend in jail for?

L. He was on probation from when he was eighteen. He stole a camera in Venice Beach off a movie set. He did like five months in county fail. He never checked back in with his probation officer, so he's back in. He'll be out pretty soon.

Q. Have you had any problems with the Police since you've been out here?

L. Just getting harassed. They stop you, run your name. They're like real racist. They say like they're investigating a crime. They just harass the kids.

Q. Do you have any aspirations, anything that you would like to do in the future?

L. Yeah, everything (laughs), go to school and take advantage of my options. I don't know anything about my career.

Q. What's the hardest part of living on the street?

L. Watching my friends and my interactions with society. I'm like a happy person, but it really tears you down watching your friends getting arrested.

TONY

Tony is a bi-racial man, black and Mexican. His head is shaved. He is thirty-one years old.

Q. How long have you been homeless?

T. About a year.

Q. What happened that you became homeless?

T. Drugs happened. I grew up in San Diego and I actually started doing speed there. I was seventeen or eighteen. I left San Diego to get away from it and I moved into this side of town. I met someone and moved out here to live with them. Once I got here I stopped doing all the drugs for a good eight years. Not all the drugs, but the ones that were really bringing me down, like speed.

About two years ago I started doing it again with some friends. It kind of snowballed from there. I was actually working a really good job, managing a coffee shop. For several years I lived alone, paid my own rent for six years. Then I started doing that. I lost my job. So, I said I'm going to be jobless for the summer. I'm going to collect unemployment and I'm not going to feel guilty about it. I had worked my ass off and I decided I needed a break.

And, during that break I started to sell drugs because it's good money. And having an abundance of it, you're able to do as much as you want. And I think that's what kinda wrecked me.

Q. Did you go to jail over that?

T. Yeah. My neighbors had been complaining that I was selling drugs. Not that they saw anything, but they just saw my coming and going. So they had five detectives follow me around town all the way from West LA down to Venice. I did it all on my skateboard or my roller blades, not by car. They were outside my house when they saw some kind of transaction. They didn't know what it was, so they stopped the guy that I just sold to, and searched him and found it. They asked did he sell you this, and he said yes.

Me and my friend went to supper right afterwards. As I was coming out, two plain clothes detectives approached me. They arrested me and searched my house. I became homeless since than. I only got ninety days as I had no criminal history, no drug problems. I only had to spend two weeks in the County jail.

Q. How long since you've been out of jail?

T. About one year.

Q. So, what have you been doing for a year?

T. Hustling a lot—kind of doing the same thing only on a different level. I'm not doing it as big time as I was doing it before. I'm just doing it to survive.

Because of the arrest I got a felony, so I can't get GR. I was told that once you've had a felony they won't help you.

I also do hair. I did do an apprenticeship in a salon. So I still do have clientele from that. I cut people's hair here and there. On the street I'll do haircuts for a couple of bucks when they need them. So that adds to my income.

Q. Where are you sleeping?

T. I don't really sleep. I mean I do sleep but during the day. I don't feel comfortable sleeping at night. There's too much going on out here. Back stabbings. I mean the homeless community in some ways can be kind of united. Other times it can be bad. If I sleep at night, my board's gone. I have to have it strapped to my body. Otherwise it's gone. So, instead I'll sleep during the day.

Nowadays, that's not so good either. They'll ticket you for sleeping in the park, if they decide to be dicks. They stop us—you can't use a shopping cart to collect aluminum cans to recycle so you can make honest money. So they force you to do the other things, breaking the law in order to make money. They don't want us here at all. And, I'm no criminal. If you look at my history, I've done nothing but work and be a good citizen.

Q. Are you going back to work?

T. I plan on going back to work. I just now decided that I'm going to take this time while I am on the streets, and not paying rent, to just go back to Cosmetology school and get my license. It's good money. It's all about interacting with people more than having talent, although that does play a part. If you can make people feel comfortable and relaxed, and then leave feeling beautiful, then they'll come back to you 'cause that's what they want.

Q. Do you do any panhandling?

T. I can't do panhandling, no way. I can't even ask people for a cigarette.

Q. Have you ever had to protect yourself?

T. No, I've never had any problems. I got about four tickets from the police for open containers, camping out, and smoking in the park.

Q. How much was your ticket for smoking in the park?

T. I have no idea. I just tossed it. I didn't even look at it, but I hear it's pretty expensive. When I was in jail they had this guy in there for five days who was mentally gone. This was for a shopping cart that he found in the alley. That's why people are doing just ten percent of their time in jail. Because they're arresting people for such stupid things—minor things that they should just let go. I mean they're not being criminal for having shopping carts. That's tax payer's dollars. And now the real criminals are getting in and out in no time.

Q. How soon are you going to go to Cosmetology school?

T. I don't know. As soon as I stop procrastinating. I'm talented. I've studied for four years, two years at a high end salon and two years at Kenneth George. I had classes every single day, shampooing all day long. And I would say "You look FABULOUS, darling!" And they love it. They LOVE it!

GENO B.

Geno is a Caucasian male. He is 5'10", has blond hair under a baseball cap, and a small beard. He is wearing shorts and a T-shirt. He is twenty-five years old.

Q. When did you first become homeless?

G. Actually when I left my house when I was fifteen. And then I was homeless for a while and staying with friends. I ended up getting a job, then getting my own apartment with a couple of friends. We then came out to California, and things turned to crap again. I came to California to make something of myself—to get a job.

Q. Where are you from?

G. Bristol, Connecticut. We came out here, me and my best friends, who ended up bailing on me. So I wasn't sure what to do after that. I went to Catholic Churches to help me out. From there I went to Job Core, trying to get off the streets. Got a good job after that for about six months. I kept doing drugs and drinking, and partying, not keeping my crap together. And then I traveled a lot. I had no constancy. I would work for six months and then go spend all my money and end up broke and on the streets again. My first trip was to Australia. Then Tokyo. I went to Taiwan, and then I came back and stayed in a shelter. In six more months I saved more money and ended up going to New Zealand.

I was working over there and making good money. I was just drinking and partying and going to strip joints, so by the time I came back I was broke again. I had enough to get a car when I got back. I had two cars. I ended up crashing one of them, and I couldn't get the other one fixed so I ended up selling it. So I was sleeping outside.

Q. How did you speak the language when you were traveling?

G. A lot of people in Japan, they talk English and stuff. New Zealand and Australia are pretty much English. You just have to go with their accent "G'day mate." They talk kind of fast so it takes awhile to understand what they're saying.

Q. Did you work in those countries?

G. I worked in both countries. In Australia I did a little bit of landscaping. I was there with a friend of mine who was an ex Police officer who I met over here in LA. He was from Australia and was just over here traveling. I had just moved up from San Diego and met him in the hospital. I got to talking with him, and there was this place called the Yes Center, which is a vegetarian commune place, but you can only stay there for thirty days at a time. At the time I was working for my friend's dad. I was doing tile and re-grouting and all that.

So my thirty days were up and the lady there said, "Why don't you move into this place for $300 a month and share with a bunch of people?" So I went there, and two days later that friend from Australia ended up coming there too. So we just started hanging out and smoking weed. So, he had sold his house and he just wanted to travel. So we went to Vegas for New Year's and traveled across country for about two years. We went to Mardi Gras down in New Orleans. We went to Daytona Beach for spring break, and we ended up back in Connecticut. Then from Connecticut we flew out of JFK airport and went to Australia. I lived there for nine months. I started doing landscaping. My friend wasn't in the Police force anymore, so he was doing private investigations and car crashes and stuff.

I used to help him do that—like measure the scenes, measure the stop signs, measure skid marks, talk to witnesses and stuff like that. So I helped him do that for awhile. Yeah, then I got in a little trouble over there. I got real drunk one night and ended up getting arrested. I had a nice car and I had to sell it. They didn't deport me although I had a round trip ticket. They just told me I had to leave. I couldn't go back for five years.

So, I came back and started living in the shelter again. Saved some money and moved to New Zealand. My friend and I met up when I was there for six days. I was making twenty bucks an hour doing construction. I was making about twelve hundred working six days a week. Everything was going good, and I applied for residency. The paper work was almost through and I had to fuck it up again. Same shit. Just talking mean and drunk. Talking shit to the cops. They said the same thing as Australia said—leave!

When I go I always buy a round trip ticket just in case something happens. I pay a little extra to keep it open for a year. So, I ended up coming back here. Things were doing okay. I was working and stuff. I was working for Labor Ready. They were giving me work every day. I had two cars at one time. I sold one car. I drove my Thunderbird all around and that got smashed. From there I started drinking like crazy and I ended up losing my passport and my birth certificate, losing all my clothes—everything. Lost all my I.D.s. I can't work until I get all that shit back. I've been trying to do whatever I can to get extra money.

Q. Have you panhandled at all?

G. I panhandle sometimes. I can't do it sober, but if I get a couple of beers in me I get the balls to go do it. Most of the time I can't just go up to someone and ask them for money.

I do neon signs. That's my trade. The reason I couldn't do it in Australia and New Zealand is because they ask for licenses and insurance and everything. Contractors' licenses and all that. See, in LA you can just go up to anybody and ask them if they want their shit fixed. And if you have the equipment they'll just say, "Go ahead and do it." And I just tell them it's going to be half-priced and give them an estimate, and bam, you make money. That's how I made enough money to go to Australia.

I had a truck; I had a Van, ladders and tools. Before I went to Australia I sold everything. Just a couple of months ago I was planning to go back to Connecticut. I got a little drunk and the next thing you know, a girl ended up stealing my wallet with my whole GR check. I couldn't work 'cause all my ID was in there.

Q. What are you doing now?

G. I've been going through Edelman's (a mental health referral). They referred me to a place in West LA where you can go to groups and get counseling. They help you with getting in the shelter. They help you with medication and stuff like that. Yeah, I'm going to give it a try because I been going all this time just thinking that things are okay. If it was okay I wouldn't be in the same situation I'm in now.

I went to jail for like twenty-one days and they gave me some medication that made me feel a lot better about myself and think a lot clearer, because I had been fogging up my mind with all the drinking. When you don't have nothing, you can't do anything. You feel helpless. I've got hundreds of friends, and we've just been getting fucked up every day. I'd wake up in a different place every day. I want to work, but I've got to take care of these problems deep down inside me. If I knew, I would try to help myself, but I've been self medicating myself for years. But yeah, I'm just hoping they can help me out to get me off of drinking, get my head clear and stuff—enough to get my shit back in order. Get my IDs and stuff.

I want to get a job for a couple of months until I can get a truck and my tools back. And just start studying for my contractor's license, where I could have a legitimate business. That's my main goal, and then travel some more. I don't like being stuck in one spot for too long. I've been back and forth to LA for five years. I've lived in San Diego for two years. I've been out here since I was eighteen.

Q. Are you basically a happy person?

G. Yeah, I'm usually in a good mood. I try not to get down on myself because when I do, and get a drink, it makes things worse. If I have a good attitude and drink, everything's cool. Everything just breezes by. I'm only twenty-five and I've been through all this shit now. I've talked to people in their forties and fifties that have fucked their whole lives up and are still in the same boat. I said I'm not going to let that shit happen to me. Just get out of this rut, and just get my shit straight.

I haven't seen my family in about three years. I wanted to go back and see them. I called my mom. I had most of the money saved for a ticket. I told my mom I needed sixty bucks for a ticket and she goes, "Ah, I can't help you." She doesn't pay any bills, and she gets free checks and shit. She doesn't work.

When I went to Australia I told my mom I'm not coming back because she stole my baseball card collection worth $50,000. She said, "Oh, I don't know what happened to it. It was in the attic." I had a little pesky fifteen year old brother that could have grabbed it and sold it on me. I had comic books, I had baseball cards, I had all kinds of collectables. I felt betrayed. I haven't seen my best friend from Australia for about a year now. It's been a year since I've been back in New Zealand. I've done alright but I've made a lot of wrong choices.

Q. What advice would you give to someone who has just become homeless and is not educated?

G. Find the right resources. Find programs. Get case management right away before you get influenced by a bunch of fuck heads on the streets. A lot of people want to bring you down 'cause they've been on the streets so long that they just want to bring you down. If you need to make some changes, then go for help in these different programs. There are plenty of programs.

If you want to get employment, start off at a place like Labor Ready. If you have the proper I.D. they get you out almost every day, and they pay you daily. It's a good way to start off. If you get with some other people who are doing that, you can afford a room. You can use these jobs as a reference to get other jobs. Basically, start off at laboring, and just ask around. Keep yourself clean. You can go to pubs down here where a lot of construction workers are they may be looking for good people.

Q. Have you had any girlfriends?

G. From time to time. You can't really meet any decent chicks on the street. You can't really meet any chicks that aren't on the street anyway because you're homeless. Wait until you get a car, a place and a job. When you start looking for these resources don't get caught in the circle of CR, OPCC, Edelman etc. None of these people know any of the resources. I found other resources. Like Traveler's Aid. You look on the internet and there's like a hundred that can help you out.

GR will say that they're the only ones who do it. There are Churches that will help you out. If you want to get back home they will take care of you. Now you have to pay a large percentage of the ticket because there are so many jerks out here. People don't want you to come up.

When you're homeless, they tag you. The cops stop you once for drinking in public, then they keep harassing you. I mean I'm not even doing nothing and they come up and handcuff me. All I had was a couple of warrants for drinking in public. I never stole nothin', I never bothered anyone. I never stole a bike like everyone else does for their drug habit. If I need money I might panhandle for a couple of beers.

JOE

Joe is a black male. He stands about 5'6" and weighs about 230 pounds. He has a moustache and is twenty-three years old. He was born here in Los Angeles.

Q. When did you first become homeless?

J. Well, I had been staying with my aunt for about six months. She was always complaining when I'd come in from work. She would say like, "Who did you bring here, I heard some girls in your room last night." I was paying like $450.00 a month to stay there. Plus, with the water bill, it came out to about $500.00 a month. She's an old lady and she was constantly giving me problems. I was working for Ralph's at the time. One night she called the Police on me. I was on probation, so she called the cops on me.

A lot of people don't realize that when you go inside jail you can die in those places. If the cops don't do it, you got the Mexicans and the white boys who try to kill you. Race wars, stuff like that. And you're trying to protect yourself. You go off in the yard one day and here's like a hundred guys coming at you with knives. You got Police and COs up there in the tower shooting at you with live ammunition. So when she called the Police on me, and the cops came out, they were like, "Do you stay here?" And I said, "Yeah, I stay here, and pay rent too." And they said, "Ma'am, we can't ask him to leave because you suspect someone else is here. Did you establish in the contract that there can be no visitors?" She said, "No." Then the cops said, "You can't tell him what to do in his own space." This happened on a Thursday. Friday I went to work and then stayed at a friend's house. I got paid on Friday, and Saturday I moved out.

Q. What kind of work did you do at Ralph's?

J. I was a deli manager. I'm not working there anymore. I had to get another job because of the strike. So I've been staying in hotels, and when I can't stay at a hotel, I sleep on the street. I've got a sleeping bag. Actually now I'm coming home to my spot, and these people are like, "Get out of here, you don't even look like you're homeless." I try to tell a lot of these people out here that just because you're homeless doesn't mean that you have to completely let yourself go.

Q. Are you working some place else right now?

J. Yes, I'm in manager training at a Coffee Bean and Tea Leaf. When I get through with that, I'll take over my own store.

Q. How did you get that job?

J. Well, I've been managing my whole career. My first management job was for the AMC theaters where I was assistant box office manager. Then I worked for Proctor and Gamble in Oxnard at their warehouse as a supervisor. Then I worked as a prep chef at Aramark. Then I worked for Ralph's. Because I always was a leader, in about six months I was promoted to manager at the service deli. I put it all down on a resume. I went to the public library where I wrote the resume. My work speaks for itself.

Q. How did you get into these places with a record?

J. Well, I just told them.

Q. What were you in for?

J. Aw, I was in for spousal abuse. On a day like today when I'm not working, to me, I always see it like this—if I wake up and I didn't make any money, then I haven't accomplished nothing. I always try to make money. If I'm not working, I'll grab my cart. I have a cart that I bought from this homeless guy for about fifteen bucks, a rubbermaid cart, and I just go about hustling cans and bottles. Right now I'm just trying to save up all my money to get off the street. That way I don't have to depend on my family because I really don't like my family because of what they did to my mother, that she died. To this day my mother still doesn't have a headstone. She died when I was like six years old. When I was twelve I was put into the system.

A lot of people you hear say that the system is bad. It's not all that bad. I was actually treated better in a lot of those foster homes than I was treated by my own family. I'm probably going to start therapy soon so I can get me some counseling. From what I've been told from a therapist is that I have unresolved anger and resentment problems.

The reason that I want to go to therapy now, and I'm taking it kind of seriously, is that I had this really nice looking girl friend. She was beautiful, funny, smart. Stimulated me intellectually. She was just great. But, like one night I just went off on her. I didn't hit her or anything. I just went off on her verbally. She was like all crying and stuff and I told her to get the hell out! That was probably the best girlfriend I'll ever have, and now I want to go to therapy because I feel that I probably won't have a good relationship until I resolve these problems. Right now I have all these girls calling me and don't even deal with them. I'm just not ready for it, not just now.

Q. Where are you sleeping these nights?

J. Behind a business. I actually rent a storage space from them. All my clothes are in storage. So now I've got like nineteen hundred dollars and like I'm looking for a roommate. I went down there to apply for Section 8 but they said I was too late. Then I found out about this program from the Salvation Army called "Beyond Shelter." But I went down there and talked to a guy and he asked to see some of my check stubs. He said I made too much money for the program.

Q. Do you have some friends out here?

J. No. I tend to believe that the best way that you deal with people when you're out here is not to make any enemies. Because first of all you're already vulnerable 'cause you're sleeping on the streets. You can be sleeping, and you know, you may have said something screwed up to somebody. That's what I told this one woman. She sleeps in my camp—an older lady. She is constantly in other people's business. I said, "You know what? That's what's going to get you killed out here."

So, my opinion is that I stay out of other people's business. I mind my own business and I tend to stay away from people. A lot of times after I pay all my bills, I'll be sitting up there hungry. And I don't have any money, but I know that they're feeding people down at this place but I won't go. I'm very outspoken and I have a big problem with these religious groups. They come and they're actually trying to help you and they give you food. But then somewhere or other in that crowd, there's always gonna be someone who wants to fight. And here these people are who are trying to help you. And I'm like "What the hell's your problem? These people are trying to help you!" They'll ruin it for everyone else.

That's what makes you not want to come back. A lot of these people are ignorant and stupid. Me personally, if I even feel like somebody's a threat to my safety, I just deal with them head on. I don't give them a chance to even get to me. If you oppose me in a threatening manner I'll put you down. That's why I don't go to these places. It keeps me out of trouble, and sometimes I have spent many nights hungry because I want to avoid trouble at all costs. I've been on probation. I'm off of probation now and I'm not trying to be back on it.

Q. What advice can you give to someone who is homeless and is not working?

J. Don't give up. A lot of people get comfortably numb. I was talking to a guy just the other day, and I was off from work and this guy was telling me, "I'm homeless." This guy comes up to me and asks, "Can I get some change to get something to eat." I said, "I'm homeless too." He says, "You sure don't look like it." I said, "You wouldn't look like it either if you took advantage of some of these programs."

A lot of times they shut down programs because people aren't using them. Okay, get a resume, go to the public library. They let you use the computer for free. The printouts are ten cents each. Little money is no excuse. Get you some resumes, make sure that you're always clean. Shave, brush your teeth, wash your face. Go spend a couple of bucks and wash your clothes. Get deodorant. Nobody wants to hire a person that smells. I've gotten many, many jobs through temporary agencies. Drop off your resume at the Temp Agency. There are other agencies like Chrysalis. They find jobs all the time.

You see these people that have been on the street for years and years. It's not because they weren't given the opportunity because there's all kinds of opportunities out here that they didn't take advantage of. They don't sit up there and say, "Okay, I got this place over here, the Salvation Army, they'll give me a blanket. They'll give me a voucher so I can get a sleeping bag. If I need some clothes I'll sign up and they'll give me fifteen dollars. I can get three outfits and some shoes. I don't have to worry about clothes. I don't have to worry about cleaning up. I can get food at these Churches over here."

These people get comfortably numb with the idea of being homeless because they don't have to accept responsibility. Some feel that they're not worth having nice things. I'm not a psychologist or anything, but these people have it in their heads that it is okay to be out there eating out of trash cans and stuff like that. You have to have some kind of dignity about yourself. They figure it's okay 'cause they don't have to work or do anything.

Q. What does the world look like to you?

J. It's a very dangerous place right now. You walk on the street and a bomb goes off. You hear about it in Israel, Africa, all down in South America. You hear about it all the time, but you never would think that something like that would happen here. But now it's like a reality. Right now my attitude as far as other homeless people, if a homeless person has a straight-up mental problem, and he's hungry and he comes up to me, and I'm making good money, I will feed him. When I go through Heaven's gates I'm not going to sit up there and answer to why I didn't feed that person. But, if I encounter a person with nothing wrong with them, and they ask me for money, I say, "I'm sorry man but I can't help you. Just like I got out there and got me something, you can do the same thing."

Few people are out here because of economic problems. I just happen to be one of those economic cases. I drink a beer every now and then, get something to eat, go to a hotel if I can afford it. A lot of people just want to get high or drunk, and I'm not gonna help you get high and drunk. I'm not with that! Some people say, "You think you're better than me." But I say, "I'm not better than you. I'm just not a fool."

RACHAEL R.

Rachael is a Caucasian woman. She is 5'4" with shoulder length blond hair in pig tails. She is twenty-one years old.

Q. I notice your tie dyed pants. Nice.

R. I did them myself. I was bleaching the white on my shoes, and I got some of the bleach on my pants. So I just got a wash cloth and did the rest of my pants with bleach to match the bleach stain in spots.

Q. How long have you been homeless?

R. Since the end of last year.

Q. What caused that?

R. An ex-boyfriend came back from Texas. I'd lived with him before. He came back from Texas and he needed a place to stay. My mom kicked me out 'cause he's black. When he came back we were like kicking it as friends. I lived in Tennessee. I had been there my whole life. I had a job making like $11.15 an hour. I had a nice car. So I said to my boyfriend, okay like we can get an apartment. And then I was like on all kinds of drugs; coke, alcohol, weed, ecstasy, and so I had been getting in trouble at work for being absent.

I also wrecked my car while I was on my way to work. I was high on meth and I had just gotten into a fight with Gary. I packed all my stuff and put it in my car. I was crying because I was mad and all that stuff. I went around this very sharp curve and over-corrected, and hit a pole. I wasn't hurt but the car was totaled.

I lost my job because of being absent so much. For the next two months we scraped by, living off the money I had saved in a savings account. I didn't draw unemployment because I had been fired from my job, so I wasn't eligible.

Then I was working at a little job at Central Park, walking back and forth every day. We started living together again, so like for two months we were just scraping by. I had just one more month on the lease. I wasn't able to come up with the rent money so he just left one night 'cause we got into a big argument. I didn't want to move back home because my step-dad drinks, and when he drinks he gets abusive.

I tried to kill myself, and then I called the cops. Then I started walking down the road, and I'm going to find my ex and I'm going to beat the hell out of him. So a Police car picked me up while I was looking for him. They took me to the hospital first to pump my stomach 'cause with all the pills I had taken I was really out of it.

I stayed there one night, and then they sent me to some mental institution. And I stayed there for like six days. They put me on medication. In Tennessee you can't really be homeless unless you're in Chattanooga, or another big city. They put me in a shelter. It was in the basement of a Church. I had to go to AA groups and all this other stuff. I started abusing my meds. I was popping like four a day when you're only supposed to take one.

In the Church they feed all kinds of homeless people, so you don't really meet the right people. I met this one guy. He said he was going to California and invited me, so I said fuck it, I have nothing else to do. I didn't even know this guy (sigh). I was so messed up that I sort of just went off with him. First we walked on the interstate, stuck out our thumbs with a sign that said "California." We got this real nice chick, and she drove us to West Tennessee. That was as far out west as I've ever been in my life. It was kind of scary.

We went to a truck stop after she dropped us off. We hit two rigs that took us through Memphis. We got another rig that took us out to—I don't remember which State. This guy had pot, so not only was I abusing Zoloft, I was smoking pot. So we hit some state and got another truck ride all the way out to El Paso.

In El Paso we had to stay in a shelter for like two days. We were on our way to Juarez on the other side of El Paso. We were going over there to party, but that didn't happen, so we kicked it in El Paso for a little while.

We went to a truck stop again, and we got a ride from there all the way to Arizona. The guy I was traveling with got mad at me 'cause I wouldn't sleep with him, so he left. He just left me with a trucker I didn't know, and the trucker smoked crack. So all the way to California I was smoking crack. It was a moving truck, and he had furniture and stuff.

In Arizona I helped him move out part of it. And when we got to California, I helped him move furniture out somewhere in Santa Monica. I forget. He was like worried about me 'cause he was a pretty cool guy. So he asked me if I wanted to stay with him. Well, I wanted to be in California, so here I am.

He took me to a shelter downtown. It's 11:00 o'clock at night at skid row and everything, so I stayed the night there, and got up the next day. I had a guitar with me, 'cause I was going to play guitar, and it didn't work, so I gave it away when I got to Santa Monica. You know I didn't know anybody, and downtown was so dirty and scary. So I said I want to go out to the beach. So I was on my way.

The truck driver gave me twenty dollars. He said he wished the best for me. So I used it to buy a pack of cigarettes and for the bus to the beach. I got on the bus and I met this guy who was all spun out on tweek (meth). By this time I've run out of my Zoloft and I hadn't smoked crack since the night before I left the truck driver. So I was sober enough to understand everything that was going on around me. This guy was scaring the hell out of me. He was talking to me the whole way.

After I got to Santa Monica I found the promenade. This guy wasn't leaving me alone. So I said, "Quit following me!" This was where the two dinosaurs were in the center of the promenade. And I hang out there, and he wasn't leaving me alone. And I met this guy who was pushing a sales cart. He told the other guy, "If you don't leave her alone I'm going to beat the shit out of you!"

That guy turned out to be a guy named Charles. He was homeless and an aspiring artist. He's really good, and he sort of took me under his wing. And like he said the first night, "You're not sleeping out on the beach. It's too dangerous. Girls like you are found in dumpsters." I thought this was a nice neighborhood. Charles was a good guy. He didn't try anything. He showed me where I could shower and get clothes and food. He said if I didn't want to sleep out in the street he could show me a shelter.

The next day I went to a place called Daybreak. It was like a woman's place. I got my shower and got my food, and I met this girl named Stephanie. She was a thug. She was like a hard core thug. Instead of staying with Charles though, I thought I'd be safer with her. Charles warned me about her. He said she was into some drama. So we hung out in the park and she showed me the promenade again, and I met some of her friends and stuff.

We left to go back to the park, and we drank and smoked pot. So, in maybe a week I started doing crystal (meth) again. So one of Stephanie's friends said, "Have you ever tried shooting it up?" I said no, so he showed me how to do it once. And after that, everybody in the park got in my face and said, "You do NOT want to do that. It's nasty, and you can catch diseases. You can get an abscess." I was high, and they were bringing me down. I said, "Okay, I'll never shoot up again." Instead I just smoked it and snorted it.

Then during this time I was doing crystal again, I met this guy. I had such a crush on him. He was sweet and smart and creative. I like to draw and stuff, so when I meet a creative person I'm drawn to them. So we hung out for some days and then him and me started dating. Then one of my friend's friends went around saying that I was a snitch and that I was a narc. Then we had a verbal fight. It could have turned physical 'cause like Stephanie's a big chick, and she could have beat the shit out of me, but she knew me, and I had been there for her and she had been there for me, so it really didn't escalate to that. She said she was going to smack me, but I got up in her face and I said, "Smack me." But she didn't.

So I quit hanging out with her, and me and Ken were hanging out every day. Even though he was on tweek and stuff, he was a really big Christian. He showed me OPCC, he showed me Common Ground, the Salvation Army, and all these different Churches. Whenever we did sleep, we'd sleep out on the beach. I think the problem was we hung out too much because we started to fight about little things. We were pretty much fighting all the time. And when you're on meth it messes with your emotions. You come out cocky, but you just sound rude. And you don't even notice that you sound rude.

I walked by this guy with a telescope looking at Mars, and I walked by and said, "What are you looking at?" And it sounded real rude. He looked me like, what's the matter with you? That's what you get for staying up two weeks, hardly eating, hardly sleeping, hardly drinking water. So it was a big emotional mess.

We broke up, so I dated his friend, Steve. I didn't want to sleep with just myself. And I didn't want to go back to Charles because I knew how he felt about it—this girl, fuck up out of her head, coming back to sleep with him just 'cause she didn't want to sleep by herself. So I was with Steve, and Steve and Ken were like really best friends. So I broke up with Steve like two or three days after I started dating him. I apologized to him and said to him, "I don't know if I was on the rebound or just using you 'cause I was scared." He was cool with it. There were rumors that I had said that Steve tried to rape me. That was in July.

Q. What are the things that brought you where you are today?

R. The reason I was hanging out with these guys all the time was because I was so messed up. I just wanted to give up. I didn't want to do anything with my life. I just wanted to do drugs and lay around. I had talked with my mom and my sister off and on. It got to the point I couldn't stand it any more.

I found a place called Daniel's Place. After I had been there for about five weeks, then I went to a mental health place. So, went there and I got sober. After I had gotten sober all my emotions calmed down. I didn't use the medication any more. It was making me like a zombie, so I quit taking it. It was like if you're not taking your meds, then you're not doing the program. I was trying to work too. They figured if I could do all this, then I had no more use for them. At the time I was making pizza in the Valley.

When I came back to the promenade all my friends seemed to be gone. So many people I had known were no longer there. I'm sober and I'm going to stay that way. I just want to get my life back on track. Charles helped me to find a job on a cart on the promenade. Then I work another cart down on the pier. I work seven days a week. Like today is the first day I had off since I started. I get $7.00 an hour. It's pretty good.

Q. Where are you staying now?//
R. One of my friends who I met when I came out here, found an abandoned house that we live in. It's a really nice house that just hasn't been sold.

Q. How does your future look now?//
R. It's looking much better. Since I came off the drugs, it is definitely looking better. I'm going to do a job program at Step-Up. I'm going to put in an application for like Starbucks. Once I have my own place and save a bunch of money, I'm going to go back to school. I want a minor in Political Science and a major in Journalism. Or, I want to know how to produce and edit CD's. I'm really into music. I want to start a band. I want to learn how to play base because I had tried the guitar. It just did not work. Basically I'm trying to find other musicians. Some people that I can get along with that have some experience. I don't have a lot of experience but I can get it, producing and editing or writing stuff.

LARRY K.

Larry is a Caucasian man of average height with dark brown hair in a pony tail. He has a full beard and is very tanned from the street. He is forty-three years old.

Q. How long have you been homeless, Larry?

L. I've been homeless a couple of times. This time it's been over a year. Time before that was in '98. I was homeless then for about six months. I'm from Dayton, Ohio.

Q. Why did you become homeless?

L. Can I ask you a question? Are you a police officer?

Q. I assure you I am not. Would you like to see some proof?

L. I just had to ask. I went to prison when I was sixteen years old. Up until I was sixteen all I knew was living on the streets and getting high and drinking. I went to prison when I was sixteen and didn't get out until I was thirty-five. When I got out I struggled with trying to make it in society, and I couldn't. I didn't know how to fit in. I felt like I wasn't a part of society. I tried to work and found out I was fearful of everything. Of people, of jobs, everything. And I realized after all those years in prison, which was almost nineteen years, I grew up there, and it's like that's all I knew. I didn't know how to live outside of that.

I've been a drinker and a drug user my whole life. I'd quit for periods of maybe six months or whatever. That was always my answer on coping with my fears, and that was to drink. I was always running away, and I always felt more comfortable by myself on the street. I didn't have to deal with other people. I feel like I'm my own best friend, my own best company. I don't know nothin' else but prison and living on the street.

Q. Where are you getting food from?

L. Ninety percent of it I get out of dumpsters. I'll go to like McDonald's or something like that after they close at night, and go through their dumpsters.

Q. Where do you sleep?

L. I sleep outside every night. I don't go to shelters cause I find I'm not comfortable doing that. I still prefer to be by myself. I slept on the beach last night. A lot of times I try to find a spot where I can't be seen by other people. It might be behind a dumpster, or in an alley, in bushes or whatever. Where ever I can lay down.

All I got is two pair of pants and some shirts. I clean up as often as I can. I'll go to the restrooms on the beach and take a shower in the sink. I'll stop in gas stations and do the same thing. When I got the money and my clothes are dirty, I'll go to the Laundry mat and wash them.

I usually wake up with the sun. I try always to have a dollar each morning so I can get a cup of coffee and smoke some cigarettes. I just keep into my head a little bit. I think a lot about the past and how I haven't been able to make anything of my life. I feel like I'm just one of those people who are just meant to live out here. Just not meant to—I don't know. Everybody's different.

I've tried to work. I've always been told I was a good worker. But those fears would set in and it's like I get anxiety attacks. Especially when I first got out of prison. I couldn't be around more than a few people before I'd get anxiety attacks. I was even on medication one time. I was diagnosed with post traumatic stress disorder from all those years I spent in prison. I was always depressed. I've been in the Salvation Army rehab programs. I did their programs twice in two different cities, six months each time. I always felt good while I was there, but again it's a structured environment. So I'd feel safe there. I felt okay there, but once I leave it's like I don't know what to do.

I don't hang with other people. I don't even talk to them unless it's to ask for directions in a new city. I got into California from Arizona ten day ago. Walked from Anaheim to Santa Monica—twenty-five or thirty miles. I've been from New York to here in the last three months. And from Ohio all the way to Florida and everywhere in between. It's like I'm looking for something but I don't know what it is. Maybe I'll know it when I see it, I don't know. Tomorrow I'll leave here. I want to go up to Oregon, then up to Washington.

Q. What are your dreams?

L. You know, I used to have dreams like that but I don't have them no more. I feel like I'm just destined to be living like I'm living. Or live in jail or whatever. I've been in relationships with women but I felt even with that I couldn't commit to a relationship. I was scared to get close to anybody. My dream was to always meet the right woman you know, and have a family cause I'm the last of my family and my name dies with me. It just seems like that's not going to happen.

I stayed out of prison for three years while I was in another structured environment for about fifteen months. Then I went back to prison again for another three and a half years. So, from sixteen to now, I spent twenty-two years in prison. Of the five years I haven't been in prison, three years of that have been in a structured environment. They were residential programs.

I thought about writing a book too, on my life, the way I've lived and had to live. The way I wasn't able to cope with things. I thought it would be a good way to cleanse my soul a little bit—kind of get my feelings on paper. Not really to sell or anything. It's kind of a journal I guess, maybe not a book. I felt like I could express it more in writing.

I am an alcoholic and I drink every day. The other day I tried not to drink because I was sick the night before. But I got the shakes so bad that by 7:00 o'clock that evening I had to have a drink. So I did drink a beer and then went to sleep. That's like something that has been part of my family for generations.

CINDY

Cindy is a forty-seven year old Caucasian lady. She has grey hair, and is 5'1". She is wearing glasses.

Q. Cindy, how long have you been homeless?

C. About fourteen or fifteen years out on the street.

Q. Where are you originally from?

C. Santa Monica.

Q. What happened that you became homeless?

C. Well, I had an alcohol problem. I couldn't work and I fell out of contact with my family. I was in a downward spiral. I just stayed out there, wandering around, finding people I could drink with.

Q. Have you had a lot of tickets out there?

C. Yeah, I just got them cleared up. I'm still homeless technically, but I'm in a transitional housing program. They allow me to stay there and save money so I can afford housing. I just recently made a decision to change my situation. I was out there sleeping by the freeway, and staying in and out of jail for all kinds of things, doing stuff mostly to get money 'cause I didn't want to work.

Q. How long have you been out of jail?

C. Ah, last time I was in jail was 2001. I went through a program called Action. It's a rehabilitation center. Alcoholics Anonymous and stuff like that. But I left there and went back to the freeway and continued drinking.

Q. Are you doing a twelve-step program now?

C. Yes. I have been sober for nine months.

Q. Are you thinking about going back to work?

C. I have a job now. I got a job through this place in Santa Monica called Chrysalis. They got me a job cleaning up trash out by the LA airport. It pays $7.50 a hour.

Q. How many hours do you work?

C. I work eight hours a day. I took the job because I went to downtown LA to see about getting my record sealed—my criminal record. So if there are any background checks it says my cases are dismissed in the name of justice. So I went and got all my paperwork for that, and I went to a homeless advisory board. I went and got signed up for that. I got elected to LAHSA (Los Angeles Homeless Authority). And they have community planning meetings there. Unfortunately not enough people showed up, so we couldn't vote on any measures or ideas we could come up with.

At the time I was staying in West LA by a liquor store (laughs). That's what caused me to become homeless, and alcohol perpetuated my homelessness. I had no motivation, no drive to do anything. I was happy to settle for drinking, the food lines, and the bushes. I had a complete disregard for hygiene, and my contact with other people or anything. A pretty bad scene. I'm glad I was able to make it out alive.

Q. Have you ever been married?

C. No, I have children though. I have four kids. I had my first one when I was twenty-seven. I had one daughter and three sons. Right after I had my third son, I started dropping out.

Q. Where are your children?

C. They're at my aunt's house. She has custody of them and stuff like that.

Q. How old are your children?

C. Fourteen, fifteen, eighteen and nineteen.

Q. Do you have any boyfriends now?

C. No, I'm just taking care of myself right now.

Q. Do you have any friends?

C. Well, I'm pretty much just working. I have to go to sleep early and get up early. I have a sponsor and an AA fellowship. And I have a few friends that I know from the shelter. I don't have any contact with the people I used to drink with.

Q. Do you get GR or SSI?

C. No, I was getting GR and then I got this job. I was getting GR for five or six years. I used to panhandle once in a while so I could drink. But I don't like to panhandle because it's too much exposure, and I didn't feel too good about myself. I'd just sit around and wait for something to come my way. I was hanging around a few people, so somebody might hustle up some money for something to drink.

Q. Have you had to see a doctor?

C. Yes, I've got hepatitis C. He said it was okay, and I get monitored. I been there twice for some blood work.

Q. How did you pay for that?

C. I go the Family Clinic. It's for free.

Q. Do you want to keep this job?

C. Not for long. Maybe another year. I'd like to go back to school. Before I started being criminal I wanted to be a lawyer. I'd like to increase my vocabulary and my writing skills. I can't stay in the shelter long. I might have to go to this other place, PATH (People Assisting the Homeless). Have you heard of that? My future is uncertain because I probably won't have enough money for a place to live.

Q. Have you ever thought of getting a roommate?

C. Yeah. I don't want to go back outside. I don't want to live that any more. I made a commitment and a decision not to.

Q. What school do you want to go to?

C. USC (laughs). A long time ago I took some classes at Santa Monica College. I still have thirty-six credits. You only need sixty for an AA. I was thinking that I was suffering from depression, when I was out there drinking and using drugs, but once I removed myself from the circumstances, my outlook became brighter.

Q. What kind of drugs were you using?

C. My drug of choice was cocaine. But I was mostly drinking. I still smoke cigarettes. I couldn't have done as well as I have without the use of these agencies. I want to give something back. I stayed out there a long time, more than most other people do. There is a whole big scope of things that are out there. Once I asked for help, people were ready to help me. It's great.

DON W.

Don is a slim, black male with a beard. He is forty-six years old. When I told Don I was writing a book, he was very interested.

D. I got a book that I'm writing, too, about poverty and stuff like that. I got three story books, "Free From The Devil's Jungle," "End Of The Rainbow," and "Poetry At Its Best." I talk about homeless life. I talk about skid row. All I do is write. That's all I do. I've been writing for about eight years now. I've only been out of prison since October. I have like four hundred and eighty-five poems and thirty-four songs, and three story books.

Q. What did you go to prison for?

D. I went to prison for possession of a controlled substance. I was framed. That was my third strike, for a dollar and twenty-five cents worth of cocaine. Thirty-five years to life. I became my own lawyer. I did over twenty-three years in prison. I got four years behind that cocaine. And then they threw a murder charge at me. They finally found out the guy who committed murder was not me. For six months they had these false allocations about me. They said I was in Lancaster when I was actually doing time in prison.

Before, I did nine and a half years for bank robbery, but this particular time I did four years. They gave me thirty-five to life, and then they found out the murders weren't mine by going through court proceedings. They offered me a deal for like six years. When it went back to court I asked them could they make a deal for four years. They said okay, and gave me four years. I've been out since 1998. I have committed no crimes since 1998. The other time they set me up in '95, I had only been out for two months. My family doesn't want to take me in, and they won't tell me what to do.

It's a struggle to survive, you know. You know, I look at society and I say to myself, they've really got things twerpted. They live a materialistic life, but they close their eyes to reality. You kind of look at people and say to yourself, you know, here they are walking these damn dogs down these little damn fence-gated community areas. They spend a lot of time and money on these dogs just to watch these dogs shit and play. But then you've got all these homeless people walking around here, you know what I'm saying? Instead of making a dog park, why don't you make a homeless park? Why don't they make a designated area called the homeless park?

You know, we bomb Afghanistan, we bomb all these places. If you notice that after they bomb, there's the big planes that come dropping cargo, cargo, cargo. Big crates of food dropping out of the plane. Food that we have never seen in the

United States. Then they bring people over here from these countries. They get number one status. One loan, one home, one everything. Can't even see your own people that have been here in America given a chance and another start. They never listen to what's really happening in life. We don't get the full concept of why this place arrives at the conclusion of where it is.

Q. How are you surviving?

D. I get food from St. Joseph's. I get it from the Lord. God blesses me in all kind of ways. I hustle cans. I go to work in Irvine. I do whatever I have to do. I drive cars at auctions. If I feel I'm getting sick of this, I catch the bus and go out to Santa Ana. In Santa Ana I work at Labor Ready sometimes. But my back's been hurting so bad living on the cement that it drains all my body nutrients. People don't realize that. The weakest part of your body goes out. My back's gone out, so I can't really work. It hurts a lot. But no matter what condition I'm in, I have to struggle to win. Just leaving something for my kids. You see, because I've had everything there is to leave.

Q. Have you ever been married?

D. No, I have never been married. I have two children. They can't stand me now because they expect more out of me. I have no domain in which to establish myself first and foremost to be what I know I am. I wrote a poem. I can write poetry better than I can talk. This is a poem I wrote. It's from one of my books.

"The Evil Within."

Here I am again, in this place they call the pen,
Trapped in evil like a long time friend.
I've been here many times before,
That's a natural fact.
But with all this evil around me,
Why do I keep coming back?

I've tried many times before,
To stay out and be clean,
But what the law has in store for me,
You know that freedom's seldom seen.

> When I look for a job, I feel funny.
> I hear the same old line,
> "Don't call us, we'll call you."
> Even your family treats you like a mummy.
> Wrapped up in disguise.
> But as long as I've been gone,
> That comes as no surprise.
>
> I wonder if there's a place for me
> To start living again,
> Whether I'm free, or in the pen.

I've got a lot of things to enjoy. Can you help me with my stories? I'm just a baby, but I've got so much to offer.

Q. I'd love to help you, but I assure you, I'm no big wig. This book about the homeless is my first attempt. I'm worrying about how to get it published.

D. I'm a homeless man, but I'm not worried. See, that's the whole thing. See, what messes a person up is their own thoughts. Just don't allow them. The hardest thing that a homeless person can do is to get on the road, because there's so many obstacles in the way, so many things that we have to do. People don't understand just what it takes to live. Do you know it actually takes all day to go and get something to eat? Do you know it takes all day to try and find some place to sleep?

Q. Do you get SSI?

D. No, I don't get nothin'. I don't want GR. I don't want nothin' but what I have to do for myself. You know I have these kids. They kicked me out. I had my son, he kicked me out. I had a woman I was staying with in Irvine. She kicked me out. You see I go to the beach for my serenity. Now that I've come out, I look at people and say to myself, "They should be where I've been."

See, these people out here haven't got no respect because they don't know what respect is. That's all right. I understand. That's what makes me somebody special. And I feel it's time I shared what I have to offer. God has provided me a way to where I can learn to translate my pain to another method. A problem's like a shadow. It will disappear. It's over with. Prepare yourself for the next one. God bless you, and good luck on your book.

(When we parted Don gave me another of his poems.)

"As I Felt Death"

Through the trees came a breeze, as I felt death,
By nights I've been gasping for my last breath.
So many things in the world that I didn't do,
I struggle for a chance, as the poor must do.
A sudden chill I would feel as I lay still,
Face down in the ground, you know it's getting real.

I didn't deserve what is happening now,
And the man on the job is suddenly gunned down.
Something's wrong in this world, something really bad,
The chemicals in the food turning people mad.
Maybe not, maybe so, how will we ever know?
United States, what can I say about your gun control?

Your constant lying to the public has really gotten old.
Life for me in the street, I think it's time I ducked,
"Cause your satellite disguise is making sure I'm fucked.
Little kids picking up guns just for fun,
Turning pages in a magazine, say "I want that one."
America, America, what a shame—As I felt death.

Survivors

FRANCIS D.

Francis is forty-two year-old black male. He is very thin, and was wearing one black sock and one white sock as I interviewed him at his apartment. He's a very likeable man.

Q. How long ago was it when you became homeless?

F. Three years ago.

Q. What happened?

F. I started drinking and the person I was living with wouldn't put up with it. I didn't want to go to my family because of my pride, so I stayed at friends houses sometimes. But most of the time I was living on the street.

Q. What were you doing for food?

F. I didn't get G.R. I went to my in-laws and I would eat there sometimes. I didn't panhandle. I was too embarrassed to do that. I knew some people that wanted to take me in, but I stayed homeless because I thought I could learn from it. My heart goes out to those who are homeless. It was very cold out there. I slept in one of those cabinets you see in building garages to stay warm. I was thirty-some odd years and I wasn't going back home. You know what I mean. It was a learning experience for me.

When I had to leave where I was living I had two dogs with me. Two champions, a male and a female. I had to take them with me for the next couple of days. I knew someone who worked in a kennel and asked them could they take the dogs for awhile. While they were in the kennel the male died. My female then got away. I didn't hold the kennel responsible. It wasn't their fault. They were doing me a favor.

I was looking out for people who were also homeless, and I was trying to comfort them, help them. You can tell if someone isn't supposed to be there. And then what little I had I would share with them. One day I hope to have my own, uh, I'm a dancer—have my own dance theater. I'm getting a grant from the government to help the handicapped people. I wish that I could root for everyone.

Well, after about a year and a half I got a job at a flower shop. I started saving my money while being a floral assistant, and then I moved into Brentwood with a man that was elderly. I lived there for two years. That's when my homelessness ended.

Q. What are you doing now?

F. I am a Floral Designer. I have two interviews tomorrow. I do flower arrangements and I also freelance as a landscape designer. I just got a call back from a shop in Beverly Hills. She called and said they really wanted me. I have good references. I also got called from another shop. Same thing. They are willing to pay me what I was asking. Most people start at these jobs at $7.00 an hour. To this day I demand $25.00 an hour because I can produce eight arrangements in an hour. So I'm making good money and they're paying me what I'm worth.

Q. What advice would you give to other homeless people?

F. That, by themselves, find what they have a passion for. We've all been blessed with many gifts and talents. Keep the Faith. Without faith you won't get it.

WILLIE M.

Willie is a forty-one year-old black woman and appears to be in great shape physically. She lives in an old apartment building in Los Angeles, with her fiancé. The apartment is kept very nicely with pictures, nice furniture, and is very clean.

Q. How old were you when you first became homeless?

W. In my late twenties.

Q. What happened? Why did you become homeless?

W. Well, I got on drugs and stuff, and I got going back and forth to jail and stuff. When I was homeless, I was in south central Los Angeles. There's not just skid row, you know. People are homeless everywhere. I found the Lord one day in jail, and went to a Christian home and got myself together. Before that I had been homeless since 1983.

My first job was in the Christian home as a secretary. I was, at that time, in a shelter for abused women and children. There was a drug program at the shelter. I was looking for a job and I became a secretary there. I was making six hundred a month.

Q. What are you doing now?

W. I'm a security officer. After being homeless for twenty years because of drugs, I needed help. I went to AA and CNA (Cocaine Anonymous) because you need help to get off the street. You can not do it by yourself. And then I found there was a God. And God helped me. But the only way you can get off the street is you've got to get help. Some people don't want to be helped, and some people are just too far gone, or scared of change. Yeah, some people are scared of change. It's like a fear. They don't want to try something new. Homeless people have got to come for help and, you know, they need to build more shelters. Shelters that will take care of them, not just send them back out at six o'clock in the morning. They should be able to stay there and get them off the street because it's cold. That's not really helping them out there.

There's a lot of people out there trying to find themselves. People need to go to Centers to get cleaned up. They can lead a productive life. People have to get their minds together. You have to see them, clean them up and counsel them. Show them that they don't have to be out in the street. Show them that they are really somebody, that there is hope.

NICK

Nick is a white male about six feet tall, with very short blond hair. He is wearing jeans and a tee shirt that's advertising something. He is forty-one years old. I interviewed him where he lives at Step-Up on Second.

Q. Nick, when did you become homeless, how did you survive and how did you get out of it?

N. My mom gave me the boot two days before my seventeenth birthday. I spent about four years in Seattle where I was in a group home with roommates. Then I went to San Francisco. I survived in San Francisco by eating out of dumpsters. Went to food kitchens, uh, was homeless in San Francisco for about two and a half years. I walked most of the way from San Francisco to Los Angeles. Got about four rides for about four miles.

I survived in Los Angeles the same way I did in San Francisco. I was homeless in Los Angeles for seven and a half years. I slept in Palisades Park in Santa Monica. I slept on tree branches. They were about as big as your arm. I laid them together and slept on them with a blanket. I used about seven or eight branches and made them into a cot. They were like oak tree branches. I also had a tarp to lay over me in case it rained. I kept a bag full of supplies.

I wore clothes I got from trash cans. I got a ticket for searching through trash, but it was just a bunch of chicken parts. I had a lot of jay walking tickets, and the offenses just multiplied. I couldn't pay the fines so I was in jail about four times for tickets.

Q. Any medical problems?

N. I never went to a doctor. I started getting SSI in 1990. Then I moved into this place, and I have been here since. (Thirteen years at this date.) I'm pretty happy with my situation now. I also do a couple hours of work a week doing barricade duty at the Farmers Market.

Q. So you're happy where you're at pretty much?

N. I consider this a satisfactory condition. When I was homeless I kept myself busy dumpster diving—extra pieces of furniture, clothes, blankets. I got a lot of supplies like that. I have found cash a few times. I just wandered around for seven and a half years in Santa Monica.

Q. What about friends?

N. I didn't have any friends, just acquaintances. Some total strangers gave me money sometimes.

NOTE: Nick now has a room at Step-Up On Second, that is all his. He is always clean shaven and his clothes are clean. He eats breakfast and supper in the community dining area.

WILLIAM B.

William is a tall, nice looking man with large hands. His brown hair is medium length, and he cuts it himself. He is forty-six years old. He has been homeless but now has housing.

Q. When did you first become homeless, and why?

W. I first became homeless when I lost my job at thirty-three. I was unemployed for one month. Then my wife and I separated and she moved out without paying the rent for about a month. That's when I became homeless. I was sleeping in my car until I got tired of it, and then let the car go and I was then out on the street. I've always been lucky. When I lost my car I found friends, and slept in the Church, and they gave me free food every day. After awhile I got a job and got back into an apartment for awhile. I then got another car. Well, I lost my job, moved out and back into my car. I started receiving Social Security. I got it because I have a mental illness.

Q. What about work?

W. When I work I always pay my taxes. I usually buy my own clothes. I have worked in Fast Food restaurants. I have driven a truck and fed animals on a farm for $1.00 a day and meals. My best life style is to go back and work for myself with my computer. I'm in reasonable good physical condition at forty-four. I want to marry again, get back into a family scenario, actually making money.

Q. Ever been in jail?

W. I have been in jail about four times. One time I was homeless and running scared this night. In essence, I stole a car to get out of town. The Police stopped me, took the car and then took me to jail.

Q. What was a typical day when you were homeless?

W. A typical day was I would walk like thirty miles one way for a day and then walk back the next day. I have always been able to buy food with my Social Security check. I once worked at a car wash. When I was twenty-one I left New York City in the spring. I had saved about $100.00. I had a bicycle and rode from New York to Kansas. It took me about twenty days with a map and a sleeping bag.

Then I got some money from my mother and rode the bus to Arizona cause my brother was living there. My brother and I aren't the best of friends, but I thought it would be okay for awhile. Got another job. Got another car and came to Los Angeles when I was about thirty-nine. I slept in my car for a month. Got rid of the car and stayed in the Salvation Army shelter for about a year. They asked me to move outside in the spring for about six months. I then found affordable housing with meals and moved in at age forty-two, and have not been homeless since.

JANE D.

Jane is a thirty-three year old Caucasian lady. She has blond hair and is wearing white pants and a straw hat with a flower as I interview her. She smiles easily and is very enthusiastic.

Q. Jane, when and why did you become homeless?

J. I first became homeless five years ago. I wasn't making enough money to pay the rent so I had to move out into my truck. I spent four years in the truck.

Q. How were you getting food at the time?

J. I was working odd jobs but I did get some from the Clare Foundation. They had a food storage situation.

Q. Where did you shower?

J. I got some help from friends occasionally. Mostly I had a bathroom key in a resort community. So I was able to use their shower.

Q. It must have been difficult living in a truck. How did you handle it?

J. Actually when I first started out I would drive to a different location every night just so that no one would be used to seeing my vehicle. And, it's really frustrating, so it was really nice when I found out there was some private property that I was allowed to park on, that I had been given permission by a business owner so I could park on his property legally.

Q. Were you collecting Social Security or General Relief at the time?

J. No. No public assistance at all. I was not eligible as far as I know. The problem is, if you have IRAs or a savings account you're not eligible for any programs. Not until you use all the money that you have. I knew that in my situation, I had a disability that could get worse. I was in a car accident, had cognitive shortages. I could work. I could function 20% of the time and the rest of the day I'd be wiped out. I'd make a lot of errors and it wouldn't be safe to drive.

Q. When did you first find living facilities?

J. I had jokingly said to a friend, "Why don't you put in a good word for me to your landlord"? Since he was moving out of his apartment, knowing that my credit situation was going to be enough to prevent me from having an apartment. And then when I found out that the landlord actually was interested in renting to me, I looked at the apartment and realized it was probably way beyond my means.

But at that point I looked at my savings account and said okay I'd be willing to try this for one year. You know, sign the lease for one year. And if in one year I'm still not making enough money for this apartment then I'll take the next step.

I just took a risk. Then when I took that risk, my income nearly doubled almost immediately after I moved in. And by the end of the year it tripled!

Q. What kind of work were you doing then?

J. A Pet care service. I was an everything service. The problem is that there's a lot of different areas of specialization, and it's usually good if you can find a niche that others haven't cornered as well. Now I'm still doing the same thing. However, my business has grown and branched out into two other businesses. I'm really not at liberty to tell you what they are. I'm making about five times what I was making when I first moved in a year ago.

I would say that the one thing that helped me the most to get my business going—well—there were two resources that were very useful. One is operated by One Stop. In there they have access to computers, photo copy machines, Fax machines and telephones in order to get work. The problem with One Stop for me eventually was that I started doing my own business instead of looking for work. And the reason I stopped looking for work was no matter how much I excelled or how well I did in any given field or any particular job, I was always considered the best, and I'd go out for the Temp agency and I was always their star person going out.

But after three months the positions disappeared. My theory is that their health insurance would not carry me because of my accident and my medical records. I'd be at every job right down to the 90th day and then boom, I was out of there. I knew that I had to do something different. No matter how good I was they weren't going to keep me. I had six other ideas of businesses I wanted to do, and it was the last thing I had down, the animal thing, because I felt it was the business that I thought would make me the least amount of money.

I really wanted to be a normal person with a normal income in society. Friends started saying, "Hey, would you come and take care of my animal?" It just built upon itself because I was willing to try whatever was in front of me. But it really took a complete willingness to let go of every preconceived idea I had about what I thought I should be doing.

JOHN P.

John is a very handsome, caring person who will go out of his way to be kind. He is a forgiving man. He has styled short blond hair, and is a forty-two year-old gay man. This interview took place on his sailboat.

Q. How many feet is this boat?

J. Twenty-eight feet. Yeah, it's in the process of getting painted and all that crap.

Q. I understand you used to be homeless. When was that?

J. Well, I was homeless during, ah, the end of '96 and almost the entire part of '97. Prior to becoming homeless I owned a flower shop. It was a really successful business. I had cars and all that stuff. But my lover passed away, and, you know, put me into a tailspin. I got involved with the wrong people. Started doing drugs. I felt that this was the best way I could maintain my loss, maintain my life after the loss. And it just took me down big time. I mean, you, people I would let in my shop would embezzle, and I did finally get busted.

Q. For what?

J. I got busted for drugs. Meth and marijuana. I had both of them on me when I got busted. I did about three days 'cause it was my first offense. I was released on OR (own reconnaissance). When I came back to court the D.A. stuck up for me. I had to go to all these meetings: NA, AA at $25.00 a week. I hated it.

Q. Then what did you do?

J. I started out just switching back and forth, ah, I had a shop out in Glendora. I was so embarrassed of everything I first stayed there, and then I went down to Ensenada because I heard there was a camp ground down there. I stayed in the campground until they finally came to me and told me there was a two week limit on your stay there at the campgrounds. And then I had to sell my tent and all that stuff that I had to sleep in and, uh, moved into the street. I started off there and then ended up coming back to LA and, uh, stayed downtown.

One night I was in Glendora. I was meeting some people there. It was about three o'clock in the morning and I fell asleep at a Del Taco drive through. I was driving one of my friend's cars, and I had been up for like eight or nine days, and got popped and went to jail.

Q. When you were on the street, where did you sleep?

J. When I was homeless I slept anywhere I could find a place that I thought was safe. Sometimes in front of doorways of businesses. I'd get up and go before they opened the shop. I went back eventually down to Ensenada where I got kicked out. There was a public beach area and there were like these bushes out by the bathrooms, and it was kinda dug out. I got me some cardboard, put some cardboard on the ground and had a blanket.

Q. How were you getting food those days?

J. There's a lot of orange trees down there in Ensenada. I ate a lot of oranges.

Q. Were you ever on GR?

J. You know, I was on GR for I don't really know how long it was for. It wasn't very long, 'cause they wanted me to come back and forth to work at this place in Pomona 'cause that's where I eventually went to get GR. They gave me food stamps and bus tokens. I don't remember if they gave me money or not. I didn't have an address, so I guess that's why I didn't get any money. But they gave me food stamps. And then they wanted me to start working for this place, I forget what it was called, like a repayment kind of thing. Working for the City offices out there, and I never showed up.

I eventually went to this little flower shop down in Ensenada before I came back and got busted in Glendora. It was difficult to get clothes to look presentable to go looking for a job. All I did was shlepp work, cleaning buckets. But the lady gave me money to eat. That would happen once, maybe twice, a week. 'Cause I knew what I was doing from when I owned my own shop.

Q. Did you ever have to protect yourself?

J. I really never—I ran into a lot of nice people. I mean there was a few people that, you know, you got money. I never really got into anything where I got beat up. When I was at the beach I tried to fit in as best I could, which is pretty easy down there. Once my friend gave me this little 1980 Honda Civic. After I got that he let me use it for shelter. So I slept in the car the last six months of it. I would use Church parking lots. Anywhere I felt I could hide away from the Police.

Q. How did you get from there to here?

J. Well, I had the car. And I see this ad in the paper for a CNA (certified nurse assistant) program they were having at this convalescent home down in Huntington Park, right off of Main Street. So, they said they would pay for training. And I thought, "Well shit, I'm going to do this." So I started the training and got certified by the State.

I applied to AIDS Health care in Hollywood. It was about two days after applying that they hired me. And I'm thinking, "What the fuck I'm supposed to do?" I had nowhere to shower. I slept in my car and worked there. That was the Linn House on Martel that has since been closed. It's turned into an office. It was a hospice house for AIDS patients. I worked there until January, 2000. I lived in the car till I got a few paychecks. Then I rented a room at a house up in Hollywood, and it took every dime I had—$695 a month to live there.

I felt like I was rich when I moved in. It felt so good. It really saved my life getting this job and becoming a member of society again. While I was working there I went to Cosmetology school out in Glendora. I did that for about a year and a half to get through Cosmetology school. It was a tight schedule. I did that until I was able to pass the State Board and get my license. Then I started cutting hair, and that's what I do now.

Q. How did you get this boat?

J. This doctor friend I had met at AIDS Healthcare, a sweetheart. He said, "John, you need to get out of that $695 room. I found you a boat down at the Marina. All you need to come up with is $3000." I gave the guy $2000 down. That was all the money I had. Then, I paid off the rest in payments. And this has been my life ever since. The rent here is $409. As you can see, it's very small, but it's my home. I've got my little dog. I rescued him from Hollywood. He was all beat up.

DAVE W.

Dave is a white male, age forty-three. He is heavy-set, clean shaven, and has short blond hair, covered with a baseball cap. I interviewed him at a sober living home.

Q. How long ago did you become homeless?

D. Since 1987. I have been homeless on and off for fifteen or sixteen years.

Q. Why did you become homeless?

D. I first left Ohio—I was wanted by the police for drunk driving. I was paranoid because they were after me. I came out to L.A. as a fugitive. When I got out here I lived in Palisades Park.

Q. How did you get your food then?

D. In those days I just went to the free places, shelters, places like that. I slept on the street every day. I would sleep at the park. I lived for a long time up at Topanga, under the bridge. The day labor was there and I would wake up, walk up from the bridge and stand in line with the Mexican day laborers. All the Spanish guys would stand on the corner, so they call me the white Mexican 'cause I was the only white boy out there. (laughs.) I worked on a day to day basis. If I didn't feel like working I wouldn't. I was drunk most of the time.

Q. What was your typical day?

D. My average day was to wake up, collect enough cans to sell to the Mexicans so I could get one full beer in the morning. And then I would panhandle money, or maybe working so I could get more cash to stay drunk all day. Some days if I just had a pack of Bugler (roll your own cigarettes), and a dollar I was fine with that too. I've been in AA for fifteen years now, in and out, but this last time since 1999 I've been sober. I stopped being homeless for good in 2000.

Q. What made you go to AA?

D. I was court ordered. Well, they put me in County jail for a month and a half. And then the Marylyn foundation, it's a program here, for ninety days, and that's what this house is affiliated with. But, see, I left here and went back to Ohio for a year and a half. I haven't worked for fifteen years straight, resume wise I had nowhere to live, nowhere to get phone calls, no clean clothes, you know? Who would hire me, you know? I had applied at about ten places and they called me up at Burger King, and it wasn't about where you worked before. They said, "When can you start"? And that opened the whole working world for me. They did the same thing for me here at the coffee shop.

When I was back in Ohio I worked for Burger King and then I worked for another Burger King and then I went to work at the Ponderosa Steak House. The Ponderosa ripped me off for some over time—twenty hours!

Q. Where were you living then?

D. I lived with my sister. I rented her basement, and they were like really controlling over me. I was like I'm thirteen years old. Then I found out I still had a warrant from when I left sixteen years before, and I thought—damn, they could come and git me anytime. I wasn't willing to go to jail though after sixteen years for drunk driving. So I came back to Southern California. I came back last year 2002. I was on SSI for the alcohol and drugs, but I guess the President ended all that. And I'd get on GR from time to time, but I'd mess up some kind of way. Sometimes I would just sign up to get the food stamps.

Q. Did you have some police trouble out here?

D. Yeah. Very near the end of my drinking career I remember the cop in Santa Monica. He said, "Damn, Mr. W., you were in our jail last year thirty-three times." That was like drunk in public or drunk and disorderly. But I never thought I had a problem (laughs) and was never willing to give sober life a try. I was driven by fear. I just didn't know how to live sober.

Q. What are you doing now?

D. I work at a food and beverage. It's a food service. I work at a small coffee shop. It was part time, but they caught one of the workers stealing money that was in management, and they gave her hours. So I'm almost full time there now. I usually work two jobs at once, and I was gone twenty hours a day. Then that one job ended and then I got a Christmas job and then I got this job which is almost forty hours a week.

Q. So, what is your situation here?

D. This is a sober living house. When I came back to Los Angeles I was having trouble trying to find a place to live because I had money in the bank. And I'd see these numbers, and I'd call them and they'd have their answering machines on. I was still homeless for a week when I came back here. I mean I didn't want to pay $60.00 a night for rent so I just slept on the street. Boy, after about a week of that I have had enough of that! It was just not being able to take a shower when I wanted you know, and just having a space of my own, a space to store my stuff. They're really fixing up this house here where I live. They're building a new back porch and new electricity. They've already fixed the foundation. They're doing some plumbing. Yes, this is a nice house. I have a checking account now, and I'm thinking about starting a savings account.

Q. So you don't see yourself going back on the street?

D. No, I don't. I would only do that as a last resort. But like, why would I? I'm sober now. Going back, it's not normal behavior. I'm in the process of looking for a new job. I feel at this job they're taking advantage of me because I'm a good worker. I've been there every day. I've never called in sick, and that's just the way I am. I always show up. I'm responsible, and it's like I do all the work. It's like they sell doughnuts now. I make the doughnuts, I sell the doughnuts. They moved the ice cream thing in there. So I sell ice cream now. It's a coffee shop, and you know they don't sell ice cream in a coffee shop. I open the restaurant, I close the restaurant. The other kids are there but they don't do the work I do, and they're getting paid the same as me. So, I think it's time to move on.

Q. Any thoughts about the future?

D. In the future I think I'd like to maybe go to college, find a wife, have the American dream. But I know everything takes time you know? I never knew what I wanted to do. I still don't. I'm just thankful for what I've got. I just stay sober. I got money in the bank. I've got fresh clothes. I got a job. That's something to me.

ROBERT H.

Robert is a very large, easy going, fun, black male who smiles easily while talking and relating his story. He is dressed in jeans and a nice shirt. Robert is thirty-five years old. He was homeless for six or seven years, and now is off the streets. I interviewed him at a center for the homeless.

Q. How long ago did you become homeless?

R. I would say that I became homeless at age twenty-eight.

Q. What would you say caused it?

R. Well, I was going through a lot of being in a major depression and a lot of abuse from my family and so-called friends. I mean I just felt like no one accepted me. I was treated like a black sheep. So I decided to leave. I was in Cleveland, Ohio actually, and came out here to California. I lived with my cousin to get away and start dealing with my mental illness and the trauma. He was related to my father. When I got out here he did what my father did, telling me what to do.

I'd be working at this garage twelve hours getting paid 60 bucks. I'm like "Wow, man, is this the only money I get?" My cousin said, "You are living at my house. That's room and board." It was chaos, so I left there. I got frustrated with everything, the way he was treating me so I walked from 52nd and Vermont all the way downtown to skid row. And that's where it began.

Actually I was on skid row and I didn't even know I was on skid row. I called my mom to send me some money, cause I love my mom. Me and my mom are very close. And I'm telling her that I have to clean up the bathroom at the Mission, the Union Rescue Mission, and I had to put on all these gloves. I told her, "You should see the people down here. They're all pushing around carts. They're living in cardboard boxes. It looks like a jungle down here. Guys over there doing drugs, down on the concrete drinking. They're nothing but a bunch of homeless people down here." My mother said, "Don't you know where you at? You in skid row!" At the time Mom was watching Geraldo on TV. They were showing the homeless people in New York and then in California. She said, "You on the nickel. That's called skid row downtown, L.A." I had heard about it, but I never thought I would be on it.

Q. How long were you there?

R. Believe it or not, I was down there eight months.

Q. What did you do?

R. Well, there were a couple of nights I had to stay outside when I didn't have enough money to get a room. I used to sleep with one eye open. I feel that God sent his angels down to protect me. It was live and learn there. I stayed at the

Frontier Hotel, one of the roughest hotels ever. People get thrown out the windows for doing drugs there. I came out to the Santa Monica Beach in '97. All new surroundings. I like it here.

So I catch the bus back downtown, and somebody had broke into my room. The latch is upside down, the room had been ransacked. They took my silver. I love silver. I left $350 in my stash. You see I found out that someone could get into your room by slipping their California I.D. into the latch. I really didn't pay it no mind, but one day, like I said, I came out here to Santa Monica just to get away from down there and when I got back is when I noticed my room had been broken into. I went down and filed a Police report. They said they can't do nothin' about it. "You didn't see nobody, no witnesses." I had to take it as a loss. I went back upstairs, packed up my belongings. I had just one big bag, a duffle bag, got back on the number 4 and came back here to Santa Monica. Being out here is more safer than sleeping in L.A.

Q. Did you panhandle here?

R. You know I did a couple of times. I really didn't like to because I felt ashamed. It was like a guilt thing. It's really not me. I kept some odd jobs every now and then. I worked at the cold weather shelter for a little while. I've worked at the Farmers Market out here some Wednesdays. I always managed to keep a little change in my pocket to buy the necessities or for doing some things I enjoy like going to the movies or for buying something to eat so I wouldn't have to beg for it. And that's what panhandling is to me. When I did I was fortunate. I used to get like $20 in 30 minutes. They used to give me $5 and $10 and change. I mean schooo! Sometimes people used to give me what they had left over from their dinner trays, steaks, lobsters, fish. I didn't like the promenade though. There was too many people.

Q. How did you keep clean?

R. I was, thank God, showering at the Salvation Army. At the SAMO shelter they had a shower program. People would come in off the streets. When I would wake up, put away my cardboard and blanket, I could go freshen up and shave. I wanted to look presentable if I wanted to go out on a job hunt. If I made like 300 bucks I would be probably inside a hotel half of the month. The rest half month I had to struggle as you would say. But, oh, thank God for the Salvation Army cause that place provided a lot of opportunities and hygiene stuff for the homeless so you didn't have to go around stinking and stuff.

Q. This brings you around to now. How did you get a job and get yourself off the street?

R. Oh, ah, I got my first job through a friend of mine. This person got a Section 8 (affordable housing). She's not able to clean up and cook for herself so she asked me to be her inner care home service worker. So I agreed and she was telling me one day when I was cleaning up, "You know what—I went to Starbucks and they helped me get my life together. So, why don't you go? You've been through a lot of trauma." She said if she hadn't opened up and asked for help, she wouldn't have her apartment.

I want to feel better. I don't want to be depressed for all my life. I felt like I wanted to get my life back together. You have to deal with life on life's terms, move through this depression and feel better. I have a case worker at this center I go to. I have a psychiatrist who I see now, and a social worker. They are all helping me deal with what I went through and know that I'm a survivor of all the things I've been through, and I can help others.

Q. Where are you living now?

R. I'm living with my friend who got the Section 8. If you don't mind me adding—throughout the years 1998 and '99 and 2000, I would go home for Mother's Day. Like I say, I love my mom. I would stay a couple of weeks with the family and then come back out here. California really did change me in a good way, after all the abuse I had in Ohio. I feel like I've found myself out here, and I'm gonna make it out here. I have a Section 8 voucher going through now.

Q. Do you have any plans for future work you're going to do?

R. Yes, I would probably like to be a facilitator at the Center here. The people here commend me on my contribution to the groups here. They even talk about me at staff meetings. This really makes me feel good. My self confidence is up. I don't have to depend on any system like Social Security of General Relief. I just want to get my apartment and I think I can handle the rest. Maybe I will be an Intern here. I feel better when I work for my money. I've been off the streets now for 8 months. I don't want to go back to the cardboard condo.

The Community

I was curious as to how various businesses were affected by the homeless, so I interviewed several owners and managers, and Police. For the most part, they asked that their names not be used.

A Tobacco Store

You know, in our business we deal with them. Fortunately, or unfortunately, ten percent of my customers are homeless, and ninety percent of those people are nasty. They smell bad. They don't know how to talk. They don't know how to treat you. Any time you treat them good, they don't care. They just go their ways. And ten percent of them are very nice people. Respectful, I love them. I take care of them as much as I can. If they need sometimes money, they are out of money, I know that they will give me back. I give them something that they need. A small amount just to make sure that everything's alright. And you know that ten percent are respectful and we try to do something for them. But about the others, seventy-five or eighty percent of them are nasty, crazy, and they smell bad all the time or steal something. I lose a lot of stuff because they steal. They come here to buy something and they steal stuff. And, they have mental problems. We've got to do something for those people because they are mentally ill. That is my view about them.

A Candy Store

Q. Do the homeless give you any problems?
A. Sometimes they do, but not really often. Sometimes they shop lift. Just kind of not being cool.

An Eating Establishment

Q. Do the homeless people give you guys any trouble?
A. We do have occasional problems. They'll come in and pass out. People have to step over them. I've had them jumping over the counter, being belligerent.

A Book Store

Q. Hello, do you work here?
A. Yes, I do.
Q. Do you guys have any trouble with homeless people here?
A. We don't have any problems I want to speak of, no.

A Gift Shop

Q. How do you feel about homeless people?
A. There are a lot of homeless people here. Of course we feel sorry for them, but for our business—I wish we could help them. People come to our store and they have to see them, it is bad for our business. They come into the store and they smell bad. We feel bad for them, but there is nothing we can do for them. The government should do something about these people. I wish the government could find a job for them, or anything.

Restaurant

Q. What do you experience from the homeless in the area?
A. We have problems, but not from all of them. There's the certain regular ones, they like mark their territory on every street. We have one lady who comes in and asks all our customers for money. Or she'll pee right in front of our restaurant. She took a shit one time on the corner of our shop right in the alley. I haven't seen her in awhile.
Q. Are there more?
A. There are several, but it's not them really coming in, it's more they sit outside and they're just yelling. Some are bad for business, some are not. We think it's bad for business but maybe our customers might not. You know what I mean? Some people are lenient towards them. They are used to living with it so they don't mind.

Sometimes they'll come in and spit on us. They spit on one of our workers. Sometimes it's hard but most of the time we don't have that many problems. This morning I guess, one of them took a piss in front of our door and no one noticed it. And then I came to work about noon and everyone is like clearing away from that area. Then I smelled it. They'll just piss wherever they want to. Maybe if they had more bathrooms, or like a shower at the beach where they could shower at. They have them in Hawaii. The bathrooms are always open. Here, the bathrooms are never open.

Doughnut Shop

Q. Do you get many homeless people here?
A. Yes, we get a lot.
Q. Have you had any problems with them?
A. Yes, sometimes. Sometimes people who have mental problems who aren't taking their medication, sometimes they give you a lot of trouble.
Q. What kind of trouble?
A. Sometimes they give some customers a bad time. They might push the customer and start speaking bad words.
Q. When do you see the homeless people most?
A. Very early in the morning and very late at night. I've had a lot of people drunk here. Sometimes I have to call the Police. I am very passionate for the homeless people. Like I know they don't have a job. Sometimes I give them a job for awhile.

Supermarket

My interview here was with Julio, the guard.
Q. How do you feel about the homeless people?
J. I have all kinds of problems. Stealing food, this goes on every day, all day long. I have to watch them when they come in. I have to tell them to get out of here. They go in the men's room and take a bath. They are in there for a long time. The floor is all wet and there's paper all over the floor. I have to tell them to get out of here. All kinds of problems, you name it. They come in drunk, bother the customers. They say like, "I'm in line, what do you want to do, I don't want to go." Yep, they're terrible. There's nothing you can do. Nobody is going to change that. I've been a guard for thirty years now. They choose to be that way, except the mentally ill.

I've talked to a few of them once in awhile. Just to see what they've got to say. I ask, "How long have you been doing this?" They say, "Oh, about ten years." I ask, "Are you mentally ill?" They say, "NO!" I ask, "Well, why do you do it?" They answer, "I don't care about anything." See what I mean? They choose that. They'll say like, "I had a good job. I was making twenty dollars an hour and then I had this girlfriend and then I started smoking marijuana and then alcohol and then da da da da." I say, "Excuse me, don't you know that alcohol and marijuana don't mix?" They'll say, "Yes, I know, but I do it anyway." See what I mean?

The Police

Because most homeless people seem to have an encounter with the Police at some time or another, I wanted to find out how the Police deal with the situation. They were very courteous to me. I interviewed a Lieutenant Frank F.

Q. What are your policies regarding the homeless?

F. Now, just to make sure you understand, I can only give you the procedures or policies from Santa Monica. They're not universal. They're different for each jurisdiction, so I can only represent Santa Monica.

Q. Are there any pressures put on the Police by shop owners?

F. I don't know if they're pressures. What I would say is their requests sometimes display a little anger towards the Police because of the homeless situation. And what I mean by that is they don't want someone in a business that hasn't bathed in two or three weeks. You know, who is eating food from a trash can, to walk in their store or place of business when other customers are there. Nobody wants that. Nobody wants to invite them to their house. There are times when they want them to be arrested when, unfortunately, it's not a crime to be dirty and not a crime to be hungry at this time.

Q. Is there pressure to move them out of Santa Monica?

F. No.

Q. What are the problems that they create for you in the Police Department, and how do you deal with them?

F. One of the things that we find is that there're crimes that are misdemeanor crimes related to homeless individuals. Some of these are urination or defecation in public, drinking in public and, you know, theft of recycling materials and things like that. Those are the crimes generally associated with the homeless, although we do not track crimes per groups. We don't have any way of going back and seeing how many homeless people did you arrest last year. However, general calls for service that we get from citizens' complaints are crimes related to that. Although they are involved in other things, those are some of the homeless type crimes.

Q. What other things are they involved in?

F. They are involved in burglaries, robberies, street robberies, assaults, things like that. It's not that homeless people only do just these types of crimes. We have them doing all sorts of crimes, both misdemeanors and felony crimes.

Q. Do the homeless cause physical damage to property?

F. I think it's like anyone, if they're doing a crime of destruction, yes they do. But it's not just the homeless people. You have people who do malicious mischief. They might break out a light pole. It's not only the homeless, but other individuals as well.

Q. Santa Monica has a reputation for being lenient on the homeless. Is this true or false?

F. I don't think they're lenient on the homeless. What I think is the city has a policy of trying to help homeless people. They have set money aside for funding social programs and things like that, that other communities don't do. And, just because there's money set aside, it attracts the homeless. They've been without an ordinance for feeding, and the city has allowed feeding to occur, so that attracts homeless. So, lenient, I don't think that's the word. I think they're more caring and concerned about the homeless population.

Q. Do you ever have to take them to jail for their own protection?

F. We don't take people into custody for that. No. Hand cuffs are always put on individuals, not just the homeless, but anyone for their protection. And that protection is that as they're driving in a Police car, or they're walking toward a Police car, because sometimes people have a change of mind and then decide they want to fight with the officer, but when they're handcuffed that likelihood is decreased. We don't treat any homeless or individuals differently. Everybody's treated the same. Our procedure is that all felons are handcuffed and then misdemeanors are generally handcuffed. And I would say that probably 99.8% of the people are handcuffed when they are arrested at all times.

Q. Do you ever use the homeless as informants?

F. No.

Q. How disruptive to the community are the homeless?

F. I think that the homeless population by nature is that they don't have a place to bathe and shower. They don't have a place to change clothing or don't have an assortment of clothing. I think they're disruptive to the community because of their sightlines. But other than that, it's not a crime not to change clothing. It's not a crime not to take a shower. Some of them just do not have that, and that's why some of the social programs that the city does have, gives them the opportunity to change clothing and bathe.

Q. Is there anything you might know about as far as getting more public restrooms, and possibly showers available?

F. I don't know of anything new. I know that the city has worked closely with the Salvation Army and Samoshel because they do offer showers there. They also have clothing. OPCC is another organization that the city works closely with. They provide not only clothing but also health care and medical care. One of the things that we have here is a homeless liaison team where we have four officers dedicated to working with the homeless, not only to focus on issues of crime, but also issues of social services. So if an officer from the homeless team runs across someone that may need medical care, or has questions in regard to where to get a shower and all that, we provide the literature and provide that information. They have those outlets and we can direct them to them.

Q. Have you had any personal dealings with the homeless?

F. I think that every Police officer in this community has had contact with the homeless throughout their career.

Q. Do you have any interesting stories you could relate about the homeless?

F. We find that not all homeless people are uneducated. We've found homeless that at one time were movie stars, actors, actresses. We find some that are well educated, have masters and PHD degrees. And then something in their life has caused them to be displaced and then become homeless. So we find a wide variety of people that yesterday were living in a nice home, owned their own cars, and had their own businesses, and because life was not as generous to them as others, now they are in the position of finding themselves homeless.

A lot of them are educated. A lot of them have families that have money. Some went to great schools. I think that the average person looks at a homeless person like a bum. If you look deep down inside you will find that a lot of them are homeless because of economic changes in their business and their fields that have forced them to no longer be able to work. They have medical issues, so now they are in a position that they no longer have a job, and they can't pay their bills. They can't pay the rent. They can't pay the mortgage, so the next stop is that they're living on a bench.

So that's why we don't come with the attitude that being homeless is a crime, because it's just a bad turn of society that has taken place with an individual. The Chief of Police in this organization has taken time to work with not only the organization but with other social organizations in this city, because any of us could be homeless tomorrow. We have employees here that get injured and can never come back to work. Fate doesn't take care of them. Nature might say tomorrow that you're homeless and out on the street with no clothes, no nothing. So we keep that in mind.

Not everybody is a criminal. There is a fraction of them that is a criminal element, just as there is that element in society. All people should know that they have the fourth amendment.* They all have the constitution. They all have the protection of the law just like you and I. And just because they don't bathe, and smell, doesn't change the law for them.

THE FOURTH AMENDMENT

The right of the people to be secure in their persons, houses, papers, and effects, against unreasonable searches and seizures, shall not be violated, and no warrants shall issue, but upon probable cause, supported by oath or affirmation, and particularly describing the place to be searched, and the persons or things to be seized.

Summary

It is a poor assumption that the homeless are mostly drug users or alcoholics, soulless leeches on society. Admittedly, some are. But many are otherwise, the product of unemployment, a failed or poisonous relationship, or loss of a supporting anchor to their lives. As well, there are those who are mentally ill, too often unrecognized as such, despised and ignored, left to fend for themselves in the tortuous, terrifying world of their imagination that can only be alleviated by medical care unavailable to them.

I did not find much apathy among the homeless. They come from all corners of the United States. They are as diverse as the rest of America. Despite differing backgrounds, education and personalities, I encountered extremely few who did not want to get off the streets, back into society's mainstream. Most dream of it. Few have any means to accomplish this. Given the harshness of their situation, it is, for most, almost impossible to do. They're in a whirlpool sucking them down and down into defeat.

Back in the days of the depression of the thirties, they were called hoboes, and it was understandable why so many people were in such a situation. But today our economy is doing well, and there is no excuse for so many to be without food and shelter, and most importantly, legitimate hope.

About the Author

Robert Greene was born in 1952 in New York City. He's lived most of his life in Santa Monica, California. He attended Santa Monica High School and Santa Monica College, after which he served a tour of duty in the U.S. Navy. He is presently a licensed Massage Therapist.

0-595-33710-4

LaVergne, TN USA
29 December 2010

210529LV00001B/127/A